custom crocheted sweaters

custom crocheted sweaters

MAKE GARMENTS THAT REALLY FIT

DORA OHRENSTEIN

 **LARK CRAFTS**

An Imprint of Sterling Publishing Co., Inc.
New York

WWW.LARKCRAFTS.COM

SENIOR EDITOR
Valerie Van Arsdale Shrader

TECHNICAL EDITOR
Karen Manthey

EDITORIAL ASSISTANT
Thom O'Hearn

ART DIRECTOR
Megan Kirby

DESIGNER
Connie Poole

JUNIOR DESIGNER
Meagan Shirlen

ILLUSTRATOR
Orrin Lundgren

PHOTOGRAPHER
Scott Jones

STYLIST
Jodi Kahn

COVER DESIGNER
Chris Bryant

Library of Congress Cataloging-in-Publication Data

Ohrenstein, Dora.
  Custom crocheted sweaters : make garments that really fit / Dora Ohrenstein. -- 1st ed.
      p. cm.
  Includes index.
  ISBN 978-1-60059-798-5
  1. Sweaters. 2. Crocheting. 3. Crocheting--Patterns. I. Title.
  TT825.O35 2011
  746.43'4--dc23
                              2011013893
10 9 8 7 6 5 4 3 2 1

First Edition

Published by Lark Crafts
An Imprint of Sterling Publishing Co., Inc.
387 Park Avenue South, New York, NY 10016

Text © 2012, Dora Ohrenstein
Photography and Illustrations © 2012, Lark Crafts, an Imprint of Sterling Publishing Co., Inc.

Distributed in Canada by Sterling Publishing,
c/o Canadian Manda Group, 165 Dufferin Street
Toronto, Ontario, Canada M6K 3H6

Distributed in the United Kingdom by GMC Distribution Services,
Castle Place, 166 High Street, Lewes, East Sussex, England BN7 1XU

Distributed in Australia by Capricorn Link (Australia) Pty Ltd.,
P.O. Box 704, Windsor, NSW 2756 Australia

If you have questions or comments about this book, please contact:
Lark Crafts
67 Broadway
Asheville, NC 28801
828-253-0467

Manufactured in China

ISBN 13: 978-1-60059-798-5

For more information about custom editions, special sales, premium and corporate purchases, please contact Sterling Special Sales Department at 800-805-5489 or specialsales@sterlingpub.com.

For information about desk and examination copies available to college and university professors, requests must be submitted to academic@larkbooks.com. Our complete policy can be found at www.larkcrafts.com.

contents

The Art and Craft of Making Garments

MANY CRAFTERS SEE their hobby as something they do for relaxation and fun. There comes a point, however, when it's obvious that to go to the next level, you have to get a little more serious about your craft. If you've got the basics down and are ready to make crocheted sweaters, you've made that leap. Welcome!

In this book, we'll not only demystify the garment-making process and offer 10 gorgeous fitted sweaters, but we'll also explore ways to adapt the patterns to fit your own body in just the way you'd like. Good-looking garments that fit well entail precise, quality work. If you think about other areas in your life where you excel, be it baking, sewing, yoga, or tennis, you'll recall that the early stages required concentration and dedication. The payoff was well worth the effort. For the crocheter, being able to plan and execute a beautiful sweater that you'll wear for years is an awesome, rewarding endeavor.

I've learned from many discussions that crocheters often have a real fear of making garments. Here are the likely sources:

- ❖ They don't know their body measurements.
- ❖ They don't know how to read schematics.
- ❖ They don't swatch sufficiently for gauge.
- ❖ They're uncomfortable with shaping techniques.
- ❖ They're using an unsuitable yarn, fiber, or weight.

Floating Tee

Double Trouble Shell

Shawled Collar Tunic

Each of these areas will be addressed in *Custom Crocheted Sweaters* so your fears vanish as your knowledge increases. The kind of knowledge needed in garment making is practical and applied, not theoretical; you learn as you practice your craft. This book is technical, but remember that all this *craft* is to enable you to create *art*. The more you think of garment making as an art form, the more exciting it will be, the more you will want to learn and grow, and the more tolerant you will be of mistakes along the way. Making art is demanding, but rewarding as well.

Introducing the Sweaters

The garments in this book are designed to familiarize you with the basic constructions you are likely to encounter in sweater patterns. You will learn how to use measurements and schematics to choose the right size. You will also learn how to take accurate body measurements, how to add the correct amount of ease, how to use a swatch to obtain reliable gauge, and how to translate that gauge into pattern instructions. We will work from simpler garments with limited shaping to more complex ones in order to build skills gradually and develop comfort along the way. The 10 patterns include everything from a basic tee to a fitted blazer, as well as designs that feature dropped-shoulder, raglan, and top-down constructions. Look at the various designs as learning opportunities: If you're a devotee of top-down sweaters, check out the set-in sleeve garments included here. As nice as it is to improvise a sweater—trying it on as you go—it's even better to have a sure sense of the measurements at your shoulders, bust, and neck-line before you begin.

My aim was to make the most beautiful designs I could. I also wanted these sweaters to be wear-able by women with a variety of shapes, and adaptable to a wide age group. I hope they can become

In Vest

Fiji Cardi

classics in your wardrobe. Rather than creating the projects to teach specific things, I made them first and let the designs show me what *they* could teach.

Every pattern includes a discussion of the construction technique and various lessons and classes. These are the pages to read when you are in a studying mood. The lessons are the heart and soul of understanding how garments are put together and how you can be in control. I urge you to study all of them even if you don't plan to make each sweater.

As you browse through the designs, remember that tweaks here and there can make an enormous difference: a very fitted design can be made more relaxed, a neckline can go up or down, and a different choice of yarn can change a garment's character dramatically. This is where your creativity comes into play!

Tapping Your Muse

Speaking of creativity, garment making can be approached from a number of possible directions. To consider two opposite poles, one might be creative and improvisatory, the other technical and methodical. I recommend a combination of both.

First, let's understand what sparks our quest for knowledge—our creative muse. It may be a simple desire for clothes that really fit and flatter your figure, or it may be a compelling need to bring to life an idea that's in your head. Whatever your muse, let it be your guide when working on something technical. Fall in love with a sweater first then make it something worthy of your love.

Changing Your Mindset

If you're new to garment making, consider a different mindset in your approach to your work. Every project may not be perfect, but it is a learning experience. Don't hesitate to pull out work if it hasn't turned out as planned. Fear of failure dogs many

Beau Blazer

Eleganza Raglan

Uptown

people, but the truth is that making mistakes and figuring out how to fix them is crucial to gaining knowledge in any craft.

Here are some other tips for successful garment making: Don't use expensive yarns on your first few garments. Start with simpler designs and work your way to the more advanced ones. Don't skip any of the steps described in the pattern or finishing instructions. Make sure you have all the tools needed before you begin, and be slow and deliberate in your work. Measure your work often to be sure your gauge hasn't changed. Consult the pattern's schematics to make sure you are meeting the specified measurements.

Using this Book

In addition to 10 sweater designs, there are alterations included for each pattern. Even if you don't intend to make a particular design, I encourage you to read through the steps involved with these alterations. You'll gain a firm grasp of different garment constructions—how they work with your body and your measurements—as well as how these variables relate to your favorite styles. If you study the patterns, lessons, and classes in the order suggested next, you will be ready when you want to make one of the garments in the book.

Start with one of the first three patterns—Floating Tee, Shawled Tunic, or Double Trouble. In fact,

take a good look at the tunic. There is a great deal to learn from this pattern about bust width in relation to shoulder width, a key element in achieving good fit. Then move on to a fitted-sleeve (Fiji), raglan (Eleganza), or top-down (Uptown) construction. Learn V-neck construction (In Vest), make a jacket (Beau Blazer), work a top-down variation (Shrug Hug), or try circular yoke construction (Cream Puff). Take charge of your education and build your skills from one design to the next. Remember—when you can make garments that really fit, they also flatter.

Shrug Hug

Cream Puff

Overview of
Sweater Construction

Overview of Sweater Construction

THIS BOOK EXAMINES the common construction techniques used to make sweaters. Once you understand them, most crochet patterns for sweaters or coats—or just about any top, for that matter—will be familiar to you. You will also have a grasp of how to alter the pattern if your measurements are different than those given in the sizes.

Basic Sweater Designs

Let's talk first about the basic types of sweaters. In *Custom Crocheted Sweaters* we'll explore dropped-shoulder, fitted-sleeve, raglan, top-down, and round-yoke styles.

Dropped Shoulder

The simplest sweater construction is a rectangle, with the style being called dropped shoulder. As we progress from basic to more sophisticated constructions, the rectangle is modified in various ways to become more closely tailored to the body. Rectangular sweaters can be made all in one piece; in two pieces—front and back; in three pieces—front and back in one piece, with two sleeves; or in four pieces—front, back, and two sleeves.

With no shoulder defined in this style, the top of the sweater glides over the shoulders and down the top of the arm, hence its name. Some extra fabric tends to gather under the arms with this construction. Rectangles have a multiplicity of uses and are a great way to feature complex stitch patterns.

Floating Tee (page 48) is a prime example of this construction. Double Trouble Shell (page 54) offers a variation on rectangular construction.

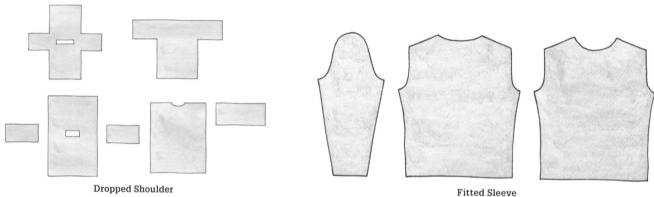

Dropped Shoulder

Fitted Sleeve

The Floating Tee is the quintessential dropped-shoulder garment.

The fitted sleeves of the Beau Blazer are a classic element used in tailored garments.

Fitted Sleeve

Tailoring with woven fabric has yielded the classic shapes we associate with more fitted garments. These shapes are typical of flat patterns where pieces are sewn together.

Note that the upper part, or yoke, beginning at the underarm, is modified to create an armhole, to which the sleeve will attach. This allows the sleeve to extend from the top of the shoulder joint to the wrist in one elegant sweep.

The neckline also departs from a pure rectangle. On the front piece of a garment, we need room for the head and neck. Because our heads angle forward on the body, the front neckline must sit lower on the torso than it does on the back.

When working cardigans or jackets, the front must be divided into two equal halves (unless asymmetry is desired). All shaping on one front piece must be a mirror image of the other.

The sleeve rectangle also grows more shaped to match the arm, narrower at the wrist and wider at the bicep. Because of the curved armhole that's been created, the top of the sleeve, called the sleeve cap, has a distinctive bell shape.

Both the Fiji Cardi (page 80) and Beau Blazer (page 90) are fitted-sleeve garments. The sleeveless In Vest (page 70) features fitted armholes, as does Shawled Collar Tunic (page 62). The latter shows how fitted armholes are constructed with vertical rows rather than the more common horizontal construction.

Raglan

Raglan

Another popular sweater construction—the raglan—has a different armhole and sleeve. Instead of following a curve from the bottom of the armhole to the shoulder edge, it proceeds at a diagonal from the bottom of the armhole to a point along the neckline. While the sleeve cap of a fitted-sleeve garment ends right at the shoulder, in a raglan design the top of the sleeve covers the shoulder and extends to the neckline.

Eleganza (page 100) is a classic raglan sweater with some special fit adjustments.

Shrug Hug is a fresh take on traditional top-down construction.

Top Down

It has become very popular to make raglan sweaters in one piece, beginning at the neckline and working from the top down. This type of construction had two influential champions in the knitting world: Elizabeth Zimmerman and Barbara Walker. It's favored because you can easily try on the working piece as you make it, to check for fit. The basic principal is to start with a circle large enough for your head and make increases at four corners, so that the sweater grows steadily until it is large enough to fit around the shoulders, then the increases continue until reaching the bottom of armhole. At this point, the torso is divided from the two sleeves and worked in the round; each sleeve is worked from its trunk.

See Uptown (page 110) for a sporty take on this style. Shrug Hug (page 118) offers a cute variation on top-down construction.

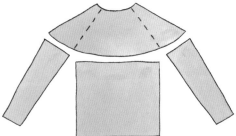

Top Down

Round Yoke

The round yoke neckline allows you to put circular designs in the yoke of a sweater, as in Fair Isle sweaters. The bottom portion of the sweater is constructed exactly as a fitted sweater. From the armhole up, it's constructed as a circle by making gradual decreases. A round-yoke sweater can also be made from the top down.

For an innovative interpretation of the round yoke construction, take a look at Cream Puff (at left).

Round-yoke construction offers lots of potential for intriguing design, as seen here in Cream Puff.

Choosing Yarns

Fingering weight bamboo rayon

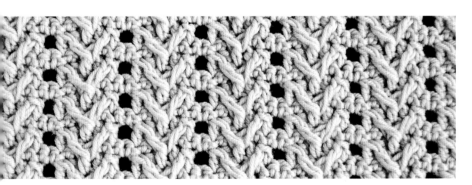

Fingering weight merino

SWEATER MAKERS MUST consider carefully when deciding on the best yarn weight. Although worsteds have become the norm for many crocheters, they are often not ideal for garments. One of the best ways to insure good crochet fabric is to work with finer yarns: DK is better than worsted, sport even better than that!

For good-looking sweaters, quality yarns are essential. Given the amount of work that goes into making one, you want it to feel great on the skin, enclose the body gracefully, and wear well over time. That doesn't mean the yarn needs to be expensive. Quality yarns are made at many price levels. A higher-grade yarn can make an enormous difference in the finished piece, affecting its beauty, durability, texture, and even color. Working with lesser-quality yarn is like using inferior ingredients in cooking, or listening to great music on poor speakers.

Choosing the Right Fiber

I recommend using lovely natural fibers, especially once you gain more experience and confidence. The fibers used in a yarn have tremendous bearing on the look, feel, and ultimately the fit of the finished piece. Along with the supple drape that some fibers give, the quality of sheen is a great enhancement to crochet fabric, giving greater dimension to the stitch patterns. Silk is a fiber that adds both luster and drape.

Soft fabric is another greatly admired attribute of clothing. Alpaca feels great on the skin and has a very attractive clinginess that counteracts crochet's bulk. This is also true of bamboo yarns and softer cottons like Pima. These pliant fibers make it possible to use a heavier-weight yarn like worsted and still get beautiful drape.

Merino is the fiber you want to choose for highlighting stitch definition. It will give a bouncy, structured look to garments. What's more, it will last.

DK weight linen, mohair, and nylon blend

DK weight cotton and silk blend

Today's upscale mohairs, especially kid mohair, are not itchy. They are incredibly light and wonderfully warm at the same time. The opposite of merino, it will soften stitch patterns. When used with a large hook and open stitch patterns, it drapes beautifully, though this is less true of the more hairy or fuzzy mohairs.

Sock yarns are a fantastic industry evolution that benefits crochet. They are usually the same as sport weight, which used to be rather scarce. Sport weight is perfect for crochet garments. With the intense craze for socks among knitters, sock yarns are now available in a cornucopia of fibers, giving crocheters great new choices.

Blended yarns—composed of several different fibers—can be a great way of obtaining the best qualities of each. You'll find some beautiful blends of silk, alpaca, merino, and cotton—perhaps two or three of these combined—that are well worth trying. Read the yarn label carefully and see what the percentage of each fiber is.

Exploring the vast variety of yarns available today is one of the greatest treats a crocheter can experience. Many of today's yarns will give you a garment that not only fits well but is also divine to wear—a creative statement of the grandest kind. It's a great feeling when you've chosen every element of the garment, from the measurements that work for you to the fabric that wraps your body most attractively.

In every design in this book, the quality of the fabric was the first consideration given to picking the yarn and weight. For most garments we will discuss substitutions and how they will affect the finished product. Of course, when substituting a different yarn, you must swatch it first to see how it will behave.

The Importance of Drape

It's well known that drape must be sought after in crochet, as it doesn't come as naturally as stiffness and structure due to the nature of the crochet stitch. Drape is the fluidity of fabric that allows it to pour over your body in elegant curves; stiff fabric makes a garment look boxy.

Use fibers that are soft. Use large hooks and open stitch patterns (garments made with lace fabric will drape beautifully). Gauge is very important for determining drape, so if you change the gauge of a design, be conscious that this will affect its drape as well. Every swatch can be tinkered with until you find the right blend of stitch definition, fabric integrity, and gauge size.

We've all seen examples of stunning crochet on the runway, in magazines, and even on the racks of department stores. High-fashion crochet is possible, and crafters can attain it too by mastering the various factors that make supple crochet fabric. Choosing the appropriate yarn is an important first step.

Worsted weight alpaca, silk, and merino blend

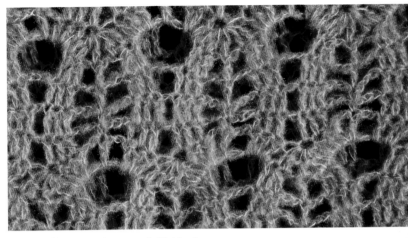

Fingering weight cashmere and silk blend

DK weight alpaca and silk blend

DK weight alpaca

Fingering weight merino and nylon blend

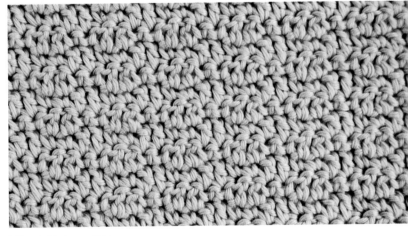

DK weight pima cotton

Measuring Your Body

TO MAKE GARMENTS that fit, you have to get cozy with your measurements. Take a deep breath, put aside the judgmental voices in your brain, and get out a flexible tape measure. If you have a friend to help, it will be easier and your measurements will be more accurate.

For this task, it's best to be clothed only in undergarments. Hold the tape measure snugly, but not tightly around you, checking each measurement carefully—if you're on your own, a mirror can be helpful. Write down all the measurements on a piece of paper, labeled carefully.

After measuring our bodies, we'll take out some sweaters that fit really well and measure them too. This step gives you important information about the fit that you prefer.

Width Measurements

Begin by measuring the circumference of your body at these crucial spots: bust, waist, and hip. Write down the exact numbers you are getting, rounded to the nearest ¼" or full centimeter. Don't pull the tape measure tight. When measuring the bust or hips, take the reading at the widest part of your body, even if it's not exactly where you think it ought to be. The waist should be measured where you are narrowest in the torso.

For those with ample bust lines, get a separate measurement for your chest, starting at the spot under the arm where the seam line falls on garments, across the chest to the opposite seam line. There may be times when good fit requires you to make the front pieces of a sweater larger than the back.

Now take a few other width measurements: right under the bust line and at the top of the hip bone (pelvis), 2"/5cm higher than the widest area of the hips. This is often where the length of the sweater ends. If you have a preference for sweaters that end at a particular length, take your width measurement right there.

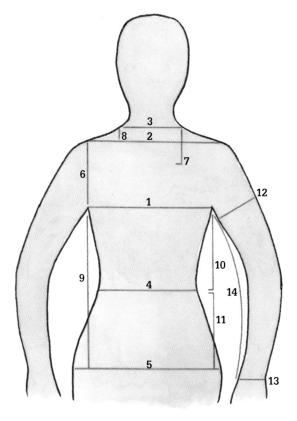

1. Bust line width
2. Shoulder width
3. Neck width
4. Waist width
5. Hip width
6. Armhole depth
7. Neckline depth
8. Shoulder slope
9. Length from armhole to bottom
10. Length from armhole to waist
11. Length from waist to hip
12. Bicep width
13. Wrist width
14. Sleeve length from armhole to bottom

Shoulder Width

Find that part of the shoulder where the clavicle ends. Measure across from one shoulder to the other. If the seamline on a jacket sits right there, it will fit very well. This is where you want the shoulder width to be on any design that's meant to be roomy across the shoulders. Anything that measures wider than this across the shoulders will droop down onto your arm. For a fitted look in a sweater, make the shoulder width about 1"/2.5cm less than this measurement.

Neck Width

Take the width measurement between the bra straps that go over the shoulders. You don't want the width of your neckline to go wider than this distance or the straps will peek out.

Arm and Wrist Widths

A measurement of great importance is the widest part of your arm, at the bicep. Also, measure your wrist circumference at the bone, as well as the width at several places you might like to see your sweater sleeve end—just under the elbow, for example.

Length Measurements

All length measurements should be taken straight down from one point to the other, never at an angle. Let the tape measure hang loosely and get a reading that lines up with the body part in question (rather than hugging the tape measure to the body, which will distort the length measurement).

Armhole Depth

Measure from the top of one shoulder to the armpit. This is your actual armhole depth. In making garments, you will always be adding about 1"/2.5cm or so of ease here, to create room for arm movement. Measure the distance from the top of the shoulder to the top of your bra band (the piece that goes all around your body). That's a good armhole depth for many sweaters, and, on a sleeveless garment, one that will not allow your bra strap to show.

Shoulder Slope

Have you noticed that the part of your shoulder close to the neck is higher than the outside of the shoulder? It's just 1"/2.5cm or so of difference, but taking this into account in garments makes a significant difference in fit. Some crochet fabric is so malleable that it may not be necessary, but in many cases there is shoulder shaping at the very top to build that extra bit of fabric. Without it, the garment rides up and the hemline will not be even. You can measure it on your body by measuring from the top of your shoulder, right next to the neck, down to the clavicle.

Precise shoulder width measurements lead to perfect fit in a sweater with set-in sleeves such as the Fiji Cardi.

In Vest features hip-to-waist and waist-to-bust shaping, so accurate measurements are important to achieve the best fit.

Torso Lengths

You may see references on sizing charts to the measurement from the neck to the waist, called waist length. For our purposes, however, it's more convenient to keep the measurements in the chest area—neck to bottom of armhole—separate from the measurement from the armhole to waist area, because that's how most sweaters are constructed. Measure from the bottom of the armhole (the top of the bra strap) to the waist; to high hip (top of the hip curve); and to low hip (the widest part of the hips). Label them armhole to waist, armhole to high hip, etc. Add any other length measurements where a sweater or tunic might end, for example, high thigh, mid thigh, and so on.

Measure the distance from your high hip to waistline. This is relevant for sweaters that have shaping from the hip to the waist. A typical measurement is 4"/10cm, and if yours is significantly different, you may have to adjust this area on patterns.

Measure the distance from your armhole to the widest part of your bust, which actually may be 1"/2.5cm or more below the armhole. Many sweaters are designed to reach maximum bust width at the armhole. As we get older, though, bust lines often fall several inches/centimeters lower than that. Ample bosoms are likely to sit lower too. Note as well the distance from your waistline to this point. These are significant numbers when working sweaters with waist shaping.

Sleeve Lengths

Now we move on to sleeve lengths, which are determined from the bottom of the armhole. With your arms hanging down at your sides, have your friend measure from the top of your bra strap under the arm down to your elbow, and again to your wrist. If you like sleeves to land somewhere in between elbow and wrist, take that measurement too.

Take the measurement called wingspan. With your arms stretched out on either side of you and with elbows slightly bent, measure from one wrist bone to the other. Take another measurement from elbow to elbow. Various factors in the upper part of the sweater—the neck and shoulder width, the height of the sleeve cap—will affect where the bottom of the sleeve actually falls on your body. Add the shoulder width plus the cap height plus the length of sleeve from underarm to get the wingspan for the sweater (these measurements are generally on the pattern schematic). Any of these numbers can be adjusted to get the sleeve length right.

Just as we considered where the widest part of the bust falls in relation to the armhole, we should determine the same thing with regard to the widest part of the arm. The wide upper arm area can be several inches in length. Measure from the bottom of your armhole (top of the bra strap) to where the wide part of your arm begins to taper—it will be several inches/centimeters long. For good fit on sleeves, we want to be sure that we hit the proper width at the right spot between the elbow and the armhole.

Now plot all these numbers on a schematic drawing that looks something like a sweater schematic. It doesn't have to be on graph paper, well drawn, or even proportional. Make it neat enough so that the numbers are easy to read, placed where you will know exactly which body part it reflects. This is a terrific reference tool you will use over and over when making and altering any sweater you plan to crochet. Add any notes about fitting you want to this page. For example, write down the various sweater lengths for high and low hip, thigh or longer, and sleeves. Once you have finished making this measurements page, scan it and load it into your computer for safekeeping.

Learn to alter length with the Shawled Collar Tunic.

Measuring Your Favorite Sweaters

This is equally as useful as measuring your body. Take a bunch of sweaters out of drawers and examine their construction. Some will have fitted sleeves, some will be raglans, and you may find some that are hard to define because the construction is more complex. Most likely you will have a range of necklines, styles, and depths as well. Keep those handy for measuring purposes.

Choose a couple of sweaters that fit like a dream. Maybe one fits great at the shoulder, another at the bust. These are the ones you want to measure. Use a hard ruler, not a tape measure. Carefully lay the sweater out flat on a hard surface. For bust width, measure the width just below the armhole. You may find the sweater is actually a bit smaller than your bust line, which means you like sweaters that fit tight across the chest. You may, on the other hand, find that your favorite sweaters are a little larger than your bust. That means you like some ease rather than a bust-hugging look. This is very personal, so don't be swayed by what you think you should like!

Another very important measure to take on a sweater with a set-in sleeve is across the shoulders, from one seam to the other. Take this shoulder width measurement on several sweaters and see what the variation is, probably about 1"/2.5cm or so from smallest to widest. See if these differences align with whether it's a heavy cardigan or a light summer sweater. The first is likely to be wider across the shoulders.

Measure the back of the neckline, the shoulder slope, and the neckline width and depth on several sweaters. Measure the armhole depth of several sweaters and get a feel for the range there, again observing how these relate to the use and/or fabric of the sweater.

On raglan sweaters you own, note the width between the two raglan seams at the neck, and also the width at the top of the sleeve. The latter figure is important if you are full-figured and want comfortable fit in your raglan sweater.

Notice that in most cases, your sweaters have waist shaping. Measure the width at the narrowest place on the sweater—the waist—and also measure the length from armpit to waist and from waist to hip. All these details can help you refine the shapes you create in your own sweaters.

Now let's measure the sleeve. Measure its width at the widest part, around the bicep, and at its narrowest part, at the wrist. Measure the length of the sleeve from the armhole to the wrist. If you have sweaters with shorter sleeves, measure the length of those as well, always from the bottom of the armhole to the end of the sleeve.

Record all the information gathered in these sweater measurements onto the schematic you made of your body measurements. Note especially the amount of ease you prefer at the bust, hip, and upper arm.

Not only can your favorite-fitting sweater tell you a lot about good measurements for crochet garments, it can also teach you a thing or two about how sweaters are constructed and how different fibers and fabrics move and stretch on your body.

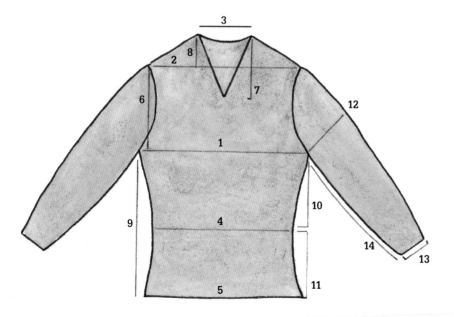

1. Bust line width
2. Shoulder width
3. Neck width
4. Waist width
5. Hip width
6. Armhole depth
7. Neckline depth
8. Shoulder slope
9. Length from armhole to bottom
10. Length from armhole to waist
11. Length from waist to hip
12. Bicep width
13. Wrist width
14. Sleeve length from armhole to bottom

Understanding Fit

MANY PEOPLE WILL LOOK at a crocheted sweater and make an instant judgment about the design. They may like the style but not the fit, adore the neckline but not its hemline, and so on. Once you understand the concepts in this book, you'll see that many sweaters need only a bit of tweaking to be made just how you'd like them. You'll understand how to check the schematics, compare the measurements to your own (to anticipate fit issues), and recognize the construction methods. Details like length, waist placement, and neckline depth are not that hard to alter and can make a huge difference in the design.

Designers must follow industry standards on what measurements are appropriate for a given size. We all know, however, that real bodies don't fit this cookie-cutter model. In fact, many crocheters are reluctant to make garments because of bad experiences with fit.

Problems with garment making are related to lack of knowledge of one's own measurements, what proportions look good on one's body, and how to choose the right size of a pattern. Crocheters don't always pay sufficient attention to the important quality of fabric drape. Without that quality, even if the sweater has the right dimensions it will look boxy and stiff rather than flattering to your body.

To make garments that fit well you need to know your body measurements; what looks good on you; and how to read the pattern and the schematics. You also need to understand the alterations that pertain to your body. When it comes to making garments, my motto is, "Ask not what your body can do for you, but what you can do for your body."

Two different length alterations are presented for Floating Tee—body length and sleeve length.

Picking the Right Size

Before you consider alterations you should start by choosing the size that best fits you and use that as a baseline. Most people start at bust width when deciding what size to make. While that's a sensible approach, it may not be the best, depending on your overall body type and shape. There are a number of considerations that should go into this decision.

Bust Width

Bust width on the schematic represents actual measurements of the garment, including any ease. When you decide which bust size works for you, make sure you are thinking about your bust size plus ease. If you like close-fitting sweaters, and are making a sweater with separate front and back pieces, you want this number to be equal to half your actual bust width, or even a bit less if you like negative ease. (Remember when we measured your favorite sweaters? This is when those measurements can really be helpful.) If you like 2"/5cm of ease, divide that number in half (1"/2.5c) and choose a bust size that is half your actual bust measurement plus half your total ease.

If you are making a sweater in one piece, the bust circumference plus ease should match your own total bust circumference plus your ease preference.

Shoulder Width

The width across the shoulders is the distance from one shoulder joint to the other. This is one of the crucial sizing areas for women. On fitted sweaters, this measurement determines where the seam between the body and sleeve of the sweater falls. Getting the right shoulder width on your sweater has a big effect on how it fits and looks.

The shoulder seam of a sweater can fall in several spots, at times more narrowly on your body or further out, to the shoulder's edge. Of course an outerwear garment like a jacket should have a broader shoulder. A cardigan with a narrow shoulder (like the Fiji Cardi, page 80) is meant to be worn over a thin shell or halter. Indoor sweaters and vests can look very nice sitting more closely on the shoulder. Unless you are making outerwear, use your actual shoulder width measurement. On vests with a narrow shoulder, the width measurement may be less than your shoulders, depending on the style. Outdoor garments can have 1" to 4"/10cm to 5cm of ease added to actual shoulder width (or even more on a coat with a broad silhouette).

Choose the size of Shrug Hug based on the neckline width.

Top-Down, Circular, and Raglan Sizes

On top-down and circular-yoke garments, no shoulder width is given since there is no shoulder seam. In picking the size, check the bust and sleeve measurements given and compare them to your own. Remember to factor in the amount of ease you like.

Shoulder width is also omitted on raglan designs. It's easiest to pick the size of raglan sweater based on bust width. If your shoulders are small compared to your bust, the sweater is likely to fit, but will be wider across the neckline than the model. To adjust this, you can add decreases along the raglan edge, a much easier task than altering shoulders on a fitted sleeve.

Choose Your Alteration

When you examine schematics and compare them to your own measurements, you will encounter the same issues repeatedly because they represent the ways in which your body departs from the so-called norm. For example, as patterns are sized up for bust width, they also gain length. But many women with ample width measurements are not tall. If that sounds like you, you'll want to get comfortable shortening patterns. By the same token, if you are slim but tall, you will want to use a smaller size that suits your bust and shoulder width, and learn how to add length to the design.

If you have fitting problems, they are likely to be one of the following:

- ✤ Your bust size is larger than your shoulder size.
- ✤ Your waist is long or short.
- ✤ You are tall compared to your width and need more length.
- ✤ You are short compared to your width and need less length.
- ✤ Your hips are much wider than your bust.
- ✤ Your bust is much wider than your hips.
- ✤ You like low necklines.
- ✤ You like high necklines.
- ✤ Your arms are much fuller on the top than on the bottom.

All these scenarios are addressed in various sections of this book. There are lessons and master classes in alteration that zero in on various strategies and techniques you will need to tailor your crochet garments for a custom fit.

Fiji Cardi offers a Master Class on Armholes and Sleeve Caps.

Demystifying Patterns

BY NOW IT'S CLEAR that sweaters are constructed from pieces, and the measurements of those pieces relate to different areas of the body. Suppose you can see from a schematic that you will need adjustments in the armhole depth and also in the length of the sweater. Each of these alterations will be in a different section of the pattern. Before you embark on any sweater project, first study the schematic well and then break down the pattern into sections, so that you can find the crucial stitch and row counts that will need to be adjusted.

Sweaters are sized and graded in sections, from one shaping point to the next. In professionally produced patterns, the sections are indicated with headings: Armhole Shaping, Waist Shaping, Neckline Shaping, Sleeve Shaping, Cap Shaping, etc. In these sections, the stitch and row counts will vary across sizes, with the different numbers for each size marching along one after the other, enclosed in parentheses. Go through the pattern and highlight the numbers that apply to your size. Look at the individual shaping sections, and check the changes in stitch counts from the beginning of shaping to the end, and over how many rows the shaping occurs. These are very important numbers that affect the fit at crucial shaping points. Be liberal with pencils and markers.

Once you learn to see the pattern in sections, it becomes more manageable. A pattern can go on for many pages and the sheer quantity of instructions, row numbers, and stitch counts can be very daunting. Make a copy of the pattern and cut it up, mark it up, paste it up—whatever makes it easier for you to comprehend it—and break it down into smaller units.

> ### note
> *Focus on the individual sections of a pattern to make it more digestible. Break it down into smaller units—cut it up or highlight different sections—whatever works.*

Bottom-Up Construction

In a typical bottom-up sweater, the first large section in the pattern is from the bottom of the sweater to its armhole. Within this section, you may see hip-to-waist shaping, then waist to bust. They may or may not be labeled, but look to see if stitch counts change between the bottom edge of the sweater and the beginning of the armhole. If there is no change in stitch count anywhere in these instructions prior to the armhole, the sweater has no waist shaping.

The next section in a bottom-up sweater is from the armhole to the neckline. Shaping at the armhole begins with the wider measurement at the bust and ends with the smaller width measurement across the shoulders. The number of rows in this section of the pattern determines armhole depth.

After the armhole, on the back of the sweater, you will arrive at the neck and shoulder-slope shaping (although some designs do not shape these areas at all). The front of a sweater will usually be the same up to the armholes, but its upper portion will include front neck shaping. In this part of the pattern, the armhole and neckline shaping are being worked at the same time. Alterations in these areas are number-intensive.

If the sweater is a cardigan, all the stitch counts on the back will be halved, and there will be a left front piece and right front piece with reverse shaping at their armholes and necklines. Remember that the left back of the sweater is shaped like the right front, and vice versa. Of course, the front pieces may not be exactly half, as front pieces may overlap or be asymmetrical. When making an alteration in a complex section of a sweater, like the upper portion on a front piece, you may wish to draw it first, using stitch symbols, to check your stitch and row counts before you begin. Designers often do this to create different sizes.

Sleeves have two main sections on a pattern, the lower portion beginning from the armhole down and the upper portion from the armhole to the shoulder (on a raglan design, from the bottom of the armhole to neckline). The lower portion determines the length of the sleeve and where it falls on your arm. The upper portion, or sleeve cap, which will be sewn into the armhole, is closely related to armhole depth.

Top-Down Construction

On top-down sweater patterns, there are three main sections: the yoke, made in one piece, which begins at the neckline and extends down to the bottom of the armhole; the torso; and the sleeves, each of which are made separately. The starting chain determines the circumference of the neckline (a measurement that's given on the schematic). Increases are then made until the proper dimensions are reached for the bust and tops of the sleeves. This section is the yoke of the sweater, and it reaches the bottoms of the armholes. The depth of the yoke determines armhole depth in this construction.

The pattern for Uptown includes sections for the yoke,
body, torso shaping, hip shaping, and sleeves.

To better understand top-down patterns, picture an expanding rectangle: The longer sides of the rectangle are the front and back; the shorter sides are the sleeves. Increases are made at both sides of each corner of this rectangle, so there are eight increase points. In the simplest top-down sweaters, the increases are the same at all eight points. For more tailored garments, there may be more increases on the front and back than on the sleeves, where less additional fabric is needed.

After the yoke is completed, the torso is worked in the round, and the stitches that belong on each sleeve are left unworked. In the first round of the torso, a bit of fabric is added for the sides of the sweater, under the arms. You will see that a few additional chains are made here to gain the extra fabric—more for larger sizes.

From the armhole down, a top-down sweater is shaped just like a fitted sweater. Since it's constructed in one piece, the shaping will be achieved internally, within rows, rather than at the sides, as is done with sweaters made in pieces.

This explanation should help you determine the important numbers in a top-down sweater. Check how many rows are used in the yoke, and if they give you the desired armhole depth. Note whether the increases differ for the front/back and sleeves. Then check how much extra fabric is added after completing the yoke—this contributes to both bust width and sleeve width. The measurements for these widths should be given on the schematic of the sweater. If they aren't, you can compute the measurements using gauge (page 34).

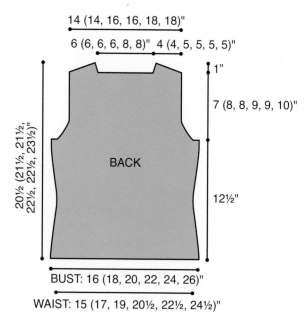

14 (14, 16, 16, 18, 18)"

6 (6, 6, 6, 8, 8)"   4 (4, 5, 5, 5, 5)"

1"

7 (8, 8, 9, 9, 10)"

BACK

12½"

20½ (21½, 21½, 22½, 22½, 23½)"

BUST: 16 (18, 20, 22, 24, 26)"

WAIST: 15 (17, 19, 20½, 22½, 24½)"

Figure 1

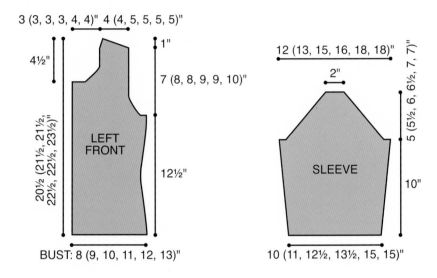

3 (3, 3, 3, 4, 4)" 4 (4, 5, 5, 5, 5)"

4½"

1"

7 (8, 8, 9, 9, 10)"

20½ (21½, 21½, 22½, 22½, 23½)"

LEFT FRONT

12½"

BUST: 8 (9, 10, 11, 12, 13)"

Figure 2

12 (13, 15, 16, 18, 18)"

2"

5 (5½, 6, 6½, 7, 7)"

SLEEVE

10"

10 (11, 12½, 13½, 15, 15)"

Figure 3

Reading Schematics

A SCHEMATIC IS A blueprint for a pattern that gives you essential information: the shapes of the main pieces used in a garment and the measurements of those pieces most relevant to size and fit. The more tailored the garment, the more numbers you are likely to see on its schematic.

To benefit from more complex schematics, you want to know what the numbers mean, how they relate to one another, and how these measurements are reflected in the design. We'll discuss the common measurements shown in a schematic, using Beau Blazer and Uptown as examples.

Bottom-Up Construction

Referring to Figure 1, the bust width is usually found at the bottom of the sweater, where it may represent the width across the hips as well, since these are often the same. When they are not the same, say in a sweater with a flared peplum, the bust widths will be shown separately. In some garments, waist width is also indicated. Since Beau is a blazer, a separate schematic (Figure 2) gives measurements for the front pieces.

Along the top of the pattern you will see the total shoulder width, the width of each individual shoulder, and the neck width. Naturally, the width of the neck plus the two shoulders should be the same as total width across the shoulders. If a garment has a wide neck, there will be less fabric covering the shoulders, since the total width across the shoulders must not change.

> ### note
> *Shoulder width—the width across the top of the shoulders—should always be the sum of the two shoulders plus the neck. Any change in neck width will result in a corresponding change in the width of each individual shoulder so the total shoulder width is maintained.*

Alongside the armhole you will see numbers representing its length, usually referred to as armhole depth. This is a length measurement and adds to the total length of the top. If the armhole depth is too short, the sweater will be tight under the arm, inhibiting you from lifting your arms. If the depth of the armhole is too long, the bottom of the sleeve will droop down on your arm. Changing the armhole depth is definitely an alteration option to master.

Just above the armhole depth measurement, you will see another number for the shoulder slope, which is the difference in height between the outside edge of the shoulder and the inside edge along the neck—usually just 1"/2.5cm or so.

You will see a number that represents the length of the sweater from the armhole down to its bottom, and another length measurement that is a total of this length plus the length of the armhole and the shoulder slope.

On the front piece (Figure 2), you will also see a figure for neckline depth, which is measured from the inside edge of the neckline down to its lowest point.

On the sleeve (Figure 3, page 31), you will see measurements for the length, from bottom to underarm. The width at the wrist (or bottom of the sleeve) is shown at the bottom edge, and the width around the bicep, or widest area, is shown at the top of the sleeve. You will also find several measurements that relate to the sleeve cap: its height, shown along the side as a length measurement, and its width, given at the top. These are important numbers if you are planning on altering the sweater.

You may also see measurements for added details such as collars, cuffs, or button bands.

Schematics for raglans look very similar to fitted-sleeve schematics. You'll notice that the armhole depths are a bit longer than on fitted sleeve garments because they start at the highest point on the shoulder, close to the neck.

Top-Down Construction

Top-down schematics tend to present measurements in a different manner, because the sweater is being made in one piece. As you see in Figure 4, on the top-down, one-piece sweater, the total neckline circumference is shown at the top. This measurement is helpful to see how low the top will sit on your neck; to check against your own measurements, take a tape measure, hold it at the number of inches/centimeters for your size, and place it around your neck. Hip, bust, and waist widths (given as half-body figures) are at the bottom, as on fitted sweaters. On the left side of the schematic, from top to bottom, length measurements are given for neckline depth, neckline to armhole base, and base of armhole to bottom of the garment. On the right side the longer line represents the total garment length and the shorter one total armhole depth. On the sleeve you see the total circumference of the sleeve at its bottom, and just above the sleeve, a line represents the length of the sleeve from the armhole base to the bottom of the sleeve.

Remember when reading a schematic that all width measurements represent half the body circumference, except at the closed edge of the sweater, at the shoulders.

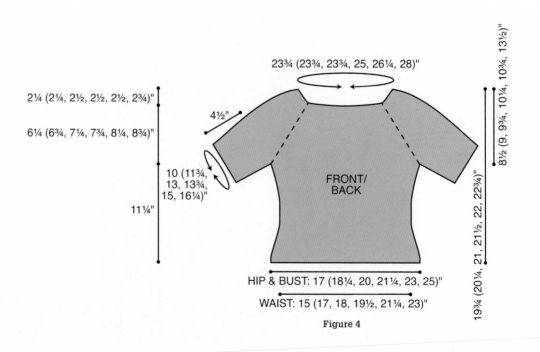

Figure 4

Here is the finished Beau Blazer; see how the schematics help you
understand its construction.

Shaping and Alteration 101

IN BOTH CROCHETING and knitting, we change the shape of the piece by adding or subtracting stitches and rows. To alter a sweater, you first need to understand basic shaping techniques, which are used to achieve fit in the garment. To make alterations, you may need to change the shaping in the pattern to achieve the desired results. In crochet, stitch patterns dictate many shaping decisions and stitch counts, as you can only create pieces to measurements that are possible with the stitch pattern and gauge chosen.

> ## note
> *Shaping achieves the desired fit in a garment; alterations involve small but significant changes in the shaping used in the pattern.*

Because knit stitches are generally smaller, knitted garments can often be tailored more precisely than crocheted garments. On the other hand, crochet fabric is more malleable, making very fine shaping less of a necessity. The larger, taller stitches of crochet are more pliant than knit stitches and have more space between them, lending crocheted fabric a particular way of molding to the body. This inherent quality means it will stretch around the body when worn. If you make the sweater to the right dimensions, roomy where it needs to be, snug where it needs to be—for your body—you will end up with a sweater that fits you beautifully.

Most shaping on garments is what we call tapered shaping, where you are working over a fairly large span of the body—from hip to waist, for example, or on a sleeve, from wrist to bicep—gradually adding or subtracting inches over the length of the fabric. The other kind of shaping, which we can call fine shaping, is in areas where curves are necessary, such as at the neckline or an armhole. Tapered shaping is typically done at the sides of garments made in pieces. When working in the round, or other one-piece constructions, it is done within rows and is called internal shaping. In any of these cases, the difference in inches/centimeters from the smallest area to the largest is calculated and then converted to stitches based on gauge. For example, if the measurement you want for the wrist is 8"/20.3cm and the bicep is 12"/30.5cm, your shaping must change by the difference—4"/10.2cm—as you work the sleeve.

The Importance of Gauge

To grasp shaping techniques and alteration methods, you must understand gauge. Gauge is an indication of what the stitches and rows measure, given the particular yarn, hook, and stitch pattern used. Without gauge, there is no way to figure out the actual size of the garment, or to match the size of a design. You should *always do a gauge swatch* before making a garment.

Start any project by making a 6 x 6"/15.2 x 15.2cm gauge swatch, using the yarn and hook recommended in the pattern. Then measure the length and width of your finished swatch. Gauge can be stated liked this: (# of stitches) x (# of rows) = 4"/10.2cm x 5"/12.7cm

Or sometimes gauge is given in terms of pattern repetitions, and will look like this:

With G hook, 4 pattern repetitions = 4"/10.2cm; 6 rows in pattern = 5"/12.7cm

To get a good gauge measurement from your swatch, I recommend a different procedure than that commonly advocated. Rather than simply measuring stitches or pattern repeats, measure the whole swatch. If it's 6"/15.2cm square, as recommended, you know how many rows and stitches it will take to make 6"/15.2cm. Now check the pattern's gauge to find out how many stitches and rows are needed for 6"/15.2cm. If you're using more stitches or rows, you need to loosen your work or use a larger hook. If your gauge used fewer stitches and rows, you need to work tighter, or use a smaller hook. Often in crochet it may be more difficult to match the row gauge than the stitch gauge, because the height of the stitches varies a lot with individual styles of stitching. If your row gauge is usually smaller than what is listed in patterns, adjust this by pulling your stitches up taller as you work. The moment to do this comes right after you draw a loop through the stitch on the previous row—pull that loop up higher before you continue the stitch and your stitches will get taller.

The Master Class in Sleeve Alteration for Eleganza presents several different learning opportunities for shaping.

Gauge and Alteration

So how does the gauge measurement relate to alteration? There are two different pieces of information given in gauge, the stitch gauge and the row gauge.

Whatever measurement you're after, you must divide it by the measurement given in the gauge. Unless your garment is worked in vertical rows, width measurements will be determined by the stitch gauge and length measurements by the row gauge.

Even if you dislike math, this is not rocket science. I promise!

Width Alterations

Let's say you want to widen the bust of your sweater by 2"/5cm; this will be a function of stitch gauge. Suppose the following:

Gauge: 6 sts = 2"/5cm; 5 rows = 3"/7.6cm

Well, that's simple and no math is even needed, because we know already from the gauge given above that we will need 6 more stitches at the bust. If you wanted to add 4"/10.2cm to the bust, you would simply multiply gauge times two—12 stitches will give you 4"/10.2cm. So far so good, right? But what if you want to add not 2"/5cm, but 3"/76.cm?

Take your alteration measurement, which is 3"/7.6cm, and divide it by the number of inches/cm in your gauge equation:

3"/7.6cm divided by 2"/5cm = 1.5.

This calculation is telling me I need 1.5 of something to reach 3"/7.6cm. What is that something? The 6 stitches in the gauge equation:

1.5 x 6 stitches = 9 stitches.

On this particular sweater, I would add 9 stitches to widen the bust by 3"/7.6cm. Any alterations, then, are calculated based on 2"/5cm segments that are 6 stitches long.

Length Alterations

Remember that row gauge is used to determine length measurements. Suppose I want to add 2"/5cm to the length of the sweater. Divide that 2"/5cm by the number in my row gauge, which is 3"/7.6cm:

2"/5cm divided by 3"/7.6cm = .666666

Now multiply that by the number of rows in the row gauge:

.66666 x 5 = 3.333333

The resulting number tells me that in order to have 2"/5cm more in length on my sweater, I have to make 3.3 rows. I can't make one-third of a row, so I either have to add 3 rows and get a little less than my desired length, or add 4 rows and get a little more. How do we decide which to do? If I want to know exactly how much length I will get if I add 3 rows, I figure it out like this: 3 rows divided by the number of rows in gauge.

3 divided by 5 = .6

This tells me I will get .6 of 3"/7.6cm if I add 3 rows, or 1⅘"/4.5cm—pretty close to the 2"/5cm I wanted. If I made 4 rows, then 4 divided by 5 = .8 x 3 = 2⅖"/6cm.

Those are my two choices, given the gauge of this sweater. It's a good example of how gauge determines and also limits the degree of fine-tuning that is possible in a crochet garment. It's really up to you whether you want a little more or a little less length. In many places on a sweater, small differences like this don't make that much difference in fit. Here are a few rules to remember about gauge, math, and alterations:

1. For width alterations, divide the number of inches/cm of the desired alteration by the inches/cm number in the gauge equation, then multiply the answer by the number of stitches in the gauge equation.

2. For length alterations, divide the number of inches/cm of desired alteration by the number of inches/cm in the gauge equation, then multiply the answer by the number of rows in the gauge equation.

3. When working a garment made in vertical rows, these equations will be reversed: width is determined by rows, length by stitches.

Always use a calculator, because you can get some pretty crazy fractions that are important to obtaining accurate results. Don't round off numbers until the last step of your calculations, when you are determining the number of stitches or rows to make.

Complex Alterations: Tapered Shaping

Let's apply this calculation method to a more advanced alteration situation, to illustrate the concept of tapered shaping. I've decided to add 3"/7.6cm more width to the sleeve, either because my arm is larger than what's on the schematic or because I like more ease in the sleeve. Sticking with the same gauge we've been using, we already figured out (in Width Alterations, on page 37) that it takes 9 extra stitches to add 3"/7.6cm. Obviously, you can't add all those stitches at once, or you will not get something shaped like a sleeve. You want a nice, gradual increase in shape, where the added stitches are distributed evenly over the whole length of the sleeve. How often you increase is called the *rate of increase*; to determine that, you need to consult the row gauge.

Gauge: 6 sts = 2"/5cm; 5 rows = 3"/7.6cm

Let's say the sleeve length from underarm to wrist is 18"/45.7cm. But I want to reach the full bicep width several inches/cm below the underarm, at a lower point than is on the pattern. Perhaps I want full bicep width at a length 15"/38.1cm from the wrist. To change the shaping I need to calculate as follows:

15"/38.1cm (total number of inches/cm) divided by 3"/7.6cm (the inch/cm number in row gauge) = 5.

This tells me I will need 5 of those 3"/7.6cm segments to make 15"/38.1cm of the sleeve. Each of those segments consists of 5 rows, so the total number of rows available to shape the sleeve is 5 x 5, or 25 rows.

The 9 extra stitches I want to add to bicep width need to be distributed evenly and gradually over 25 rows. But those stitches must be added to *both* sides of the sleeve, or my sleeve will be lopsided. Since 9 can't be divided evenly, I will round it up or down—a

1-stitch difference will not undo your beautifully calculated outcome. Knowing that the garment is bound to stretch, I will round it down to 8, which means I will add 4 stitches on each side of the sleeve. I have 25 rows to do this, but I'm going to round that also to a number that's divisible by 4 and make it 24 rows. To determine how to distribute these increases evenly, you must divide the number of rows by the number of stitches:

24 rows divided by 4 stitches = 6, which tells me that every 6 rows I will add 1 stitch to both sides of my sleeve. I will end up with a nicely tapered sleeve that has the pattern's original measurement at the wrist, but reaches the width I need—3"/7.6cm extra—at a lower point on the upper arm.

Tapered shaping is used in many areas on a garment. If the torso has waist shaping, it is used from hip to waist to decrease the size gradually, and then increase it again going from waist to bust. On raglan sweaters, it is used at the raglan edge of both body and sleeve.

Here are the steps to follow for tapered shaping:

1. Determine the number of stitches to be increased or decreased from the beginning of the tapered area to the end.

2. If the increases or decreases will be made on both sides of the piece, divide the number of stitches in half.

3. Divide the total number of rows in the tapered area by the number of stitches obtained in step 2.

4. The resulting number tells you how often to work an increase or decrease row (i.e., if your answer is 4, increase/decrease every fourth row).

Fiji Cardi offers a couple of lessons in alteration, including a Master Class on Armholes and Sleeve Caps.

When the width of a garment changes slowly, as it does on sleeves, the rate of increase is slow. That means stitches are added on minimally—usually 1 stitch at each end of the row, with several rows between the increase rows. When the width changes rapidly, so do the increases. In top-down sweaters, there is a rapid increase from the neck down.

To sum up how the rate of increases changes the shape:

❖ Increasing 1 stitch at a time along the edge makes a steady diagonal.

❖ Increasing more stitches at the edge of every row makes a steeper diagonal.

❖ Spreading increases out over more rows makes a more gradual diagonal.

Naturally, the same rules apply if you decrease instead.

When shaping is done at the sides of pieces which will be seamed, it's important to avoid sharp angles that can occur when rapid increases or decreases are used because these edges will be longer than the rest of the work. As a result, the sides will droop. To avoid this, keep the rate of increase or decrease slow—not more than 1 or 2 stitches per row on each side.

Internal Shaping

We've discussed tapered shaping, which is worked at the side edges of fabric. But how is shaping done in garments that are worked in one piece where there are no edges? To change the width of the fabric in this case, we add or subtract stitches within the row, and it's called internal shaping.

Top-down sweaters use just this kind of internal shaping. The measurement from neck to bust must change quite rapidly, and all the additional fabric must be added in the space available lengthwise—about 7"/17.8cm to 12"/30.5cm—over all sizes.

The Cream Puff cardigan (page 129) is worked in one piece and all the shaping is done internally, with stitch counts changing within the rows. What's particularly nice about internal shaping is that there is no seam to affect.

When internal shaping is used, alterations are calculated in the same way as for tapered shaping. Use the steps outlined above, but skip step 2. You will not divide the stitches in half. The increases or decreases will be dispersed within the row.

Understanding Pattern Repeats

In many patterns in this book, gauge will be given in Pattern Repeats rather than stitches. This method is used because the design is built on individual Pattern Repeats as its shaping units; decreases and increases will be made with whole Pattern Repeats, not individual stitches. Your calculations for alterations should also use them as a unit.

Calculate and Chart Your Alterations

Following the procedures described in this chapter, decide which stitch and row counts will be changed. Mark them clearly in the pattern.

If you plan to do any alterations, make a new schematic with the measurements you want. Notate it with row and stitch counts. Schematics can be very helpful in achieving the end result you want.

Measure Your Work

When making a sweater, measure often and carefully to see if you are meeting the measurements on your schematic. Even with our best intentions, gauge can change. If you are altering a design, this will also reveal any mistakes in calculations that may have crept in (it happens!).

Additional Alteration Strategies

In addition to the shaping techniques we've been examining, there are many other clever ways to alter the size of a garment. You can change the gauge, a process that is discussed in Lesson 9 (page 88). You can also fix some measurement problems by wet blocking, discussed on page 45. You can change the hook size for just a few rows to pull in the fabric, as you might do at a neckline.

Don't heed arguments that suggest one method is bad and another good. Any strategy that achieves the fit you want and doesn't compromise the functionality of the fabric is legitimate. For example, when working a complex stitch pattern, you can change to plain stitches near the edges so you can shape more easily. Edgings can be added at the bottoms to increase length, so long as they blend nicely with the stitches in the garment. Aesthetic considerations are important too.

The Bottom Line

Here's what knitting guru Barbara Walker wrote about shaping and math:

"And that, ladies and gentlemen, is all there is to shaping. Did you think it was complicated? On the contrary, it's a sort of common-sensical problem-solving, on the order of 'If Mary has ten apples…', etc. If numbers tend to make you sleepy, as they do me, you can always turn the shaping arithmetic over to the nearest third-grader—who, if he or she has been paying attention in school, can do it just as well as you or I can."

She wrote those words in 1972. I hope they are still true.

In one-piece, top-down construction in Cream Puff (seen here), shaping is done internally within the rows.

Finishing with Care

NOW THAT YOU'VE invested time and creativity into your perfectly fitted sweater, finish it with care and attention to detail.

Making Seams

Before you start making seams, label all your pieces carefully, indicating left or right, front or back. (If your pieces need to be blocked, as discussed on page 45, do so before seaming.) Leave tails at both ends of your seam. When weaving the tails in, use them to reinforce the seams on the garment's inside by turning and re-stitching them once more for a few inches/ centimeters, working into different strands than before.

The least obtrusive seam is made with mattress stitch. This seam is meant to disappear into the garment, a feat that's accomplished by weaving yarn in and out of the edge stitches. In most cases, pick up only one strand on either side of the seam. This seam is often the best choice for side seams and armholes, but not for areas where there will be stress and pull, such as the shoulder.

When working this seam, match your stitches up carefully, checking that stitch patterns are lining up at the same point on both sides of the seam. At both ends of the seam, pay special attention that they meet neatly and close well.

You can work seams either from the inside, or wrong side, of the garment or the outside, or right side. Which one looks better depends on the stitch pattern used. Working from the right side allows you to see exactly what stitches you are picking up and how your finished seam will look.

The shoulder seam must be strong. This is a good place to use a slip-stitch or single-crochet seam. Work these from the wrong side. You can also do a mattress-stitch seam and work it twice, on the outside and inside of the garment. Because this seam is worked more heavily, the fabric will become firmer.

When working a slip-stitch seam, you don't need to use the same-size hook as you used to crochet the pieces. Choose your hook based on the ease of picking up single strands of yarn on either side of your seam. Don't make the stitches so tight that they pucker the fabric.

Sleeve cap-to-armhole seams can be tricky, since you are working with two edges that are very different. These must be worked after shoulder seams are done. Pin the two pieces in place, making sure the center of the sleeve cap lines up exactly with the shoulder seam. At the bottom of the cap, where it meets the armhole, take care that the two sides close neatly and line up with the armhole seam. Begin sewing from the bottom of the

armhole, checking carefully along the way to the shoulder. Sew the armhole seams first, and then work the seam on the sleeve itself. You can use mattress stitch on the sleeve seam.

Sometimes, despite our best efforts, the two pieces to be joined do not measure exactly the same length. Luckily, the malleability of crochet fabric allows us to do an effective cheat by easing in the extra fabric on the longer side while seaming. Use safety pins to join the two pieces at crucial points; on an armhole seam, for example, pin at the bottom of the armhole and at the center of the shoulder. As you work the seam, bring the longer side in by including a bit more fabric on each stitch. For an armhole seam, up to 2"/5cm can be eased in this way—for seams along the sides of the garment, less than that. If you encounter the latter problem, it's wiser to block your pieces (see Blocking with Confidence, on page 45) so they match in length.

You can also use slip stitches to even out edges before making a seam. If the side edges are longer than the rest of the garment, or if your edges don't quite match, work a tight row of slip stitches along the longer edge to make it shorter.

After completing your seam, steam it with an iron to flatten it.

Firming Edges

Crochet fabric tends to be larger at the top and bottom edges of the work. This can be an advantage—for example, to create extra room in the hip area—but up near the neck, or at the sleeve edge, a firmer edge is desirable. Use a row of slip stitches to tighten the fabric. At the neckline, you can work successive rows of single-crochet stitches, decreasing each row, to tighten the neckline significantly.

Adding Buttons

Choose buttons carefully for crochet garments. Avoid those that are heavy, as they will pull at the fabric. Buttons with shanks are easier to work with than those without.

Crochet fabric can sometimes be too unstable to sew a button into. You can use a smaller button on the inside to sew into. Run your needle through the button on the right side, through the garment, then through the small button on the back.

In cases where the fabric seems too unstable to hold a button, see the strategy used in finishing the Shawled Collar Tunic (page 62).

Learn more about blocking to measurements
for the Double Trouble Shell in Lesson 3, page 60.

Blocking With Confidence

Blocking is part of the finishing of a project, and a great tool to master to get the precise size you want. If your pieces look great when they're done, with no curling edges, and are the right dimensions, you don't have to block at all. When you do block, do so with individual pieces before they are sewn together.

Blocking can be done with either water or steam, but each has a different purpose. Steam blocking works very well for flattening curls at the edges. Place your pieces on the ironing board, or a blocking board if the pieces are large, and hover the steam iron over them. Avoid placing the iron directly on the fabric.

Wet blocking is great for evening out stitches and getting very precise dimensions on pieces. Before blocking a piece of the garment, block a swatch to see how it reacts. Immerse the fabric in water for a few minutes so it gets totally soaked. Then roll it into a towel to absorb some of the moisture. Finally, pin it on a blocking board. Use a commercially made blocking board imprinted with a grid showing well-marked inches or centimeters.

Block your swatch without stretching it much—just square off the edges nicely. This is different than fine lace blocking for shawls. There may be instances when you will block lace for garments, but for most crochet garments, intense stretching is not necessary.

Before you block pieces, measure them. They may be about 1"/2.5cm less than the finished measurements on your schematic. Pin them out on the blocking board to the exact dimensions you want in the garment. Blocking can help cover miscalculations in measurements; you can stretch portions of the sweater and give yourself another 1"/2.5cm or so, but use this method cautiously—if you pull it out too hard, some stitches will look distorted and not match the rest of the garment.

If you don't intend to block, take into consideration the stretch factor of certain fibers, like silk, cotton, and alpaca. They will stretch with wear, so it's wise to make the finished pieces a little smaller than you intend them.

A lighter wet-block method is spritzing finished pieces with water and then pinning them on a blocking board. You won't get the full effect of evened-out stitches that a full-immersion soak gives, but it's a good method when using fabric that is apt to stretch too much, like cotton or alpaca. If you have a stubborn curl at the edge of a garment, a spritz can be more effective than steam.

If you are making a one-piece design or have a piece that's too large to fit on the blocking board, block it in sections. Wet and pin one section and let dry; repeat as necessary. Repeated wetting will have no ill effects.

Caring for Your Garments

Hanging crochet garments is not a great idea, as they are likely to stretch out of shape. Fold and store your crochet garments in a place where moths are unlikely to go.

Hand-wash a crocheted sweater in mild detergent. If you're dealing with just a small spot, use a damp towel and soap to remove it rather than washing the whole garment.

Roll the sweater in a towel to remove excess water and then dry it flat.

The most important care you can give your crocheted garments is to *wear them*. They get lonesome if left in the closet for too long. You don't want fashion styles, or your body, to change too radically while your garment lingers, waiting for just the right occasion.

The Sweaters

FLOATING TEE
dropped-shoulder construction

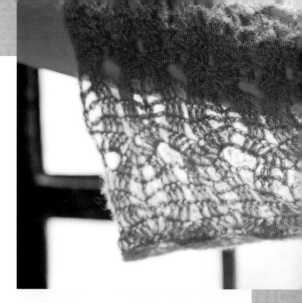

The key to creating this beautiful, fluid silhouette is using yarn with fibers that drape well.

Stitch Pattern

❖ PATTERN REPEAT (FOR GAUGE SWATCH)

Ch 39 (multiple of 12 plus 3)

Row 1: Dc2tog in 5th and 6th ch from hook (counts as dc3tog), *dc in next 2 ch, (dc, ch 2, dc, ch 2, dc) in next ch, dc in next 2 ch**, dc5tog over (next 2 ch, sk ch, next ch, sk ch, next 2 ch), rep from * across, ending last rep at **, dc3tog over (next 2 ch, sk ch, last ch), turn—3 patt reps.

Row 2: Ch 3 (counts as dc here and throughout), *dc in next 3 dc, ch 3, sk next ch–2 sp, sc in next dc, ch 3, sk next ch–2 sp, dc in next 3 dc**, ch 1, sk next dc5tog, rep from * across, ending last rep at **, dc in tch, turn.

Row 3: Ch 3, *dc in next 3 dc, ch 3, sc in next sc, ch 3, dc in next 3 dc**, ch 1, rep from * across ending last rep at **, dc in tch, turn.

Row 4: Ch 4 (counts as dc, ch 1 here and throughout), *dc in next 3 dc, ch 2, sk next ch–3 sp, dc in next sc, ch 2, sk next ch–3 sp, dc in next 3 dc**, ch 3, sk next ch–1 sp, rep from * across, ending last rep at **, ch 1, dc in tch, turn.

Row 5: Ch 5 (counts as dc, ch 2 here and throughout), sk next ch–1 sp, *dc in next dc, dc2tog over next 2 dc, ch 1, sk next ch–2 sp, dc in next dc, ch 1, sk next ch–2 sp, dc2tog over next 2 dc, dc in next dc**, ch 5, rep from * across, ending last rep at **, ch 2, dc in 3rd ch of tch, turn.

Row 6: Ch 5, dc in first dc, 2 dc in next ch–2 sp, *dc5tog over (next 2 dc, sk ch, next dc, sk ch, next 2 dc)**, (3 dc, ch 2, dc, ch 2, 3 dc) in next ch–5 sp, rep from * across, ending last rep at **, 2 dc in ch–2 sp, (dc, ch 2, dc) in 3rd ch of tch, turn.

Row 7: Ch 1, *sc in dc, ch 3, sk next ch–2 sp, dc in next 3 dc, ch 1, sk next dc5tog, dc in next 3 dc, ch 3, sk next ch–2 sp, rep from * across, sc in 3rd ch of tch, turn.

Row 8: Ch 1, *sc in sc, ch 3, sk next ch–3 sp, dc in next 3 dc, ch 1, sk next ch–1 sp, dc in next 3 dc, ch 3, sk next ch–3 sp, rep from * across, sc in last sc, turn.Row 3: Ch 3, *dc in next 3 dc, ch 3, sc in next sc, ch 3, dc in next 3 dc**, ch 1, rep from * across ending last rep at **, dc in tch, turn.

Row 9: Ch 5, sk next ch–3 sp, *dc in next 3 dc, ch 3, dc in next 3 dc, ch 2, sk next ch–3 sp, dc in next sc**, ch 2, sk next ch–3 sp, rep from * ending last rep at **, turn.

Row 10: Ch 4, sk next ch–2 sp, *dc2tog over next 2 dc, dc in next dc, ch 5, sk next ch–3 sp, dc in next dc, dc2tog over next 2 dc, ch 1, sk next ch–2 sp, dc in next dc**, ch 1, rep from * across, ending last rep at **, placing last dc in 3rd ch of tch, turn.

Row 11: Ch 3, sk next ch–1 sp, dc2tog over next 2 dc (counts as dc3tog), *(3 dc, ch 2, dc, ch 2, 3 dc) in next ch–5 sp**, dc5tog over (next 2 dc, sk ch, next dc, sk ch, next 2 dc), rep from * ending last rep at **, dc3tog over (next 2 dc, 3rd ch of tch), turn.

Rep rows 2–11 for patt.

FINISHED MEASUREMENTS
Chest 36 (40, 44, 48, 52)"/91.5 (101.5, 112, 122, 132)cm

MATERIALS AND TOOLS
Filatura di Crosa Superior (70% cashmere, 30% silk; .88oz/25g, 330 yd/297m): 3 (4, 4, 5, 5) skeins, color #30 Orchid—approx 990 (1320, 1320, 1650, 1650)yd/891 (1188, 1188, 1485, 1485)m of fingering weight yarn; **❶**

Crochet hook: 3.25mm (size D-3 U.S.)

Yarn needle

GAUGE
3 patt reps = 6"/15.2cm; 10 rows in patt = 3½"/8.9 cm

Always take time to check your gauge.

Special Abbreviations

dc2tog: [Yo, insert hook in next st, draw up a loop] twice, yo, draw through 2 loops.

dc3tog: [Yo, insert hook in next designated st, draw up a loop] 3 times, yo, draw through 4 loops.

dc5tog: [Yo, insert hook in next designated st, draw up a loop] 5 times, yo, draw through 6 loops.

STITCH PATTERN

REDUCED SAMPLE
OF SECOND SLEEVE

REDUCED SAMPLE
OF FIRST SLEEVE

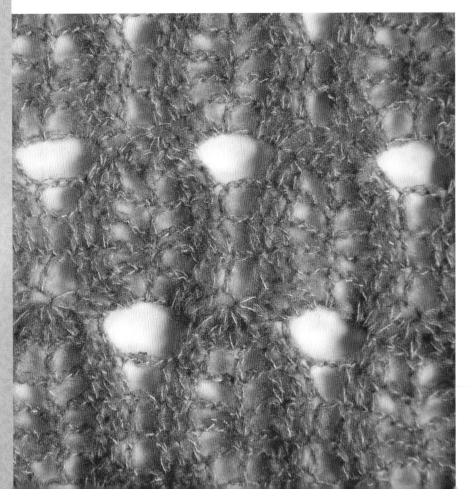

Instructions

Body (Back/Front)—make 2
Ch 111 (123, 135, 147, 159)
Work Rows 1–11 of patt; rep Rows 2–11 (3
times)—109 (121, 133, 145, 157) sts, 9 (10, 11,
12, 13) patt reps. Do not fasten off.

Sleeves
At end of same row, ch 86 (86, 74, 74, 74),
place lp on safety pin. Join a separate strand
of yarn on opposite end of same row and ch
86 (86, 74, 74, 74). Fasten off.

ROW 1 (SAME AS ROW 1 OF PATT): Pick up
dropped lp at end of last row, dc2tog in
5th and 6th ch from hook, *dc in next 2 ch,
(dc, ch 2, dc, ch 2, dc) in next ch, dc in next
2 ch**, dc5tog over (next 2 ch, sk ch, next
ch, sk ch, next 2 ch *, rep from * to * across
added ch, ending last rep at **, dc5tog
over (next 2 ch, sk ch, next dc of last row,
sk ch, next 2 dc), work in patt row 11 across
to within last 4 sts, dc5tog over (next 2 dc,
sk ch, 3rd ch of tch of last row, sk ch, next 2
ch), rep from * to * across added ch, ending
with dc3tog over (next 2 ch, sk ch, last ch),
turn—277 (289, 277, 289, 301) sts; 23 (24,
23, 24, 25) patt reps.

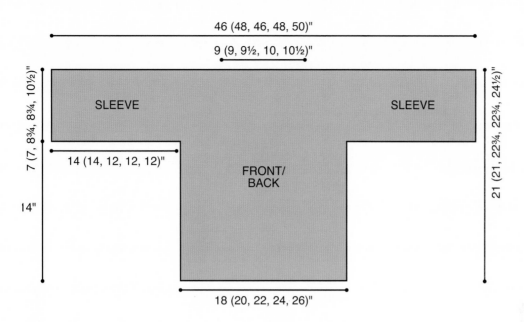

46 (48, 46, 48, 50)"

9 (9, 9½, 10, 10½)"

SLEEVE   SLEEVE

7 (7, 8¾, 8¾, 10½)"

21 (21, 22¾, 22¾, 24½)"

14 (14, 12, 12, 12)"

FRONT/
BACK

14"

18 (20, 22, 24, 26)"

Sizes S and M only:
ROWS 2–20: Rep rows 2–11 of patt (once); rep rows 2–10 of patt (once).

Sizes L and 1X only:
ROWS ROWS 2–25: Rep rows 2–11 of patt (twice); rep rows 2–5 of patt (once).

Sizes 2X only:
ROWS 2–30: Rep rows 2–11 of patt (3 times).

Top Edging

Note: This row is worked in sc to provide a firm edge. The stitch counts and placement of the stitches make the top edge flat.

Sizes S and M only:
LAST ROW: Ch 1, sc in first dc, *2 sc in next ch–1 sp, sc in next 2 dc, 4 sc in next ch–5 sp, sc in each of next 2 dc, 2 sc in next ch–1 sp, sc in next dc, rep from * across, ending with last sc in 3rd ch of tch—299 (312) sts. Fasten off.

Sizes L and 1X only:
LAST ROW: Ch 1, sc in first dc, 2 sc in ch–2 sp, *sc in each of next 2 dc, 2 sc in next ch–1 sp, sc in next dc, 2 sc in next ch–1 sp, sc in next 2 dc**, 4 sc in next ch–5 sp, rep from * across, ending last rep at **, 2 sc in next ch–2 sp, sc in 3rd ch of tch—299 (312, 325) sts. Fasten off.

Finishing

With WS of Front and Back facing, start at the bottom of the garment and sew the side seam, continuing the seam all along the bottom of Sleeve. (Recommended seam: Mattress Stitch from RS on side seams, picking up inside sts.) Since this is quite a long seam, you can use more than one strand of yarn to cover all this territory. *Remember, if you want more room on the hips, leave a 3 to 4"/7.6 to 10.2cm slit (unseamed) at the bottom, on each side of Body.*

Note: Before you work the seams across the tops of Sleeves and the shoulders, try on the garment and mark off how wide you want your neckline to be. You may find it easier to sew the shoulder seam to a point 1 to 2"/2.5 to 5cm wider than the neckline given in the schematic, but don't end off at your seam; leave 12"/30.5cm of yarn on each side with which to finish it. Now try it on again and determine exactly how close you want the neck to fit. Keep the neckline fairly wide so that the fabric will hang nicely from one shoulder point to the other and not come up too close to the neck. Sew upper sleeve seams to the marked points on the neckline.

Construction Details

FLOATING TEE IS DESIGNED for maximum fluidity in the fabric. It feels divine to wear. Large lace patterns are not often used in garments, because they're hard to shape. That's the perfect reason to use them in this very simple dropped-shoulder construction.

Simple rectangles can clothe the body beautifully if the fabric flows gracefully, draping in attractive folds. Stiff fabric will not do this, and the wearer looks packaged in a box.

The design is made in two pieces, front and back. It begins at the hip and goes straight up to the armhole, with no shaping at all from the hips to the bust—it's the same width throughout. At the armhole, the sleeves are added to the working piece by making additional chains at left and right.

After the additional chains are added for the two sleeves, the rows extend all the way from the bottom edge of one sleeve, across the body, and continue to the edge of the opposite sleeve. Please note that the vertical *height* of this section of the sweater determines the *width* of the sleeve. Remember that the number on the schematic represents

half the width of the sleeve. The small and medium, with 7"/17.8cm widths, are actually sleeves that are 14"/35.6cm wide, while those on the largest side are 10½"/26.7cm x 2, or 21"/53.3cm.

In this construction, when you finish making the sleeve you've arrived at the end of the sweater and there is nothing additional to do for neck and shoulders. How is it possible for the top edge of the sweater to be straight across and still fit nicely across the neck? The answer is the drape of the fabric. Because the neck is fairly wide, this loose fabric will not stretch rigidly across from one shoulder to the other, but will instead fall loosely between them, creating a natural neckline.

Substituting Yarn

The lace pattern used in this design can be worked at the given gauge with fingering, lace, or even certain sport weight yarns. What's more crucial is the fiber: Be sure to pick fibers with plenty of drape, such as bamboo, silk, or alpaca. 100 percent cotton is likely to be too stiff, but there are plenty of sock yarns with a mix of fibers that can work for this design.

If you like this lacy rectangular sweater, I strongly encourage you to make more than one version of it. Do you have a lace shawl you love to wear? Redo it as a tee. Use what you've learned about gauge and math to create the dimensions that work for you. This is such an easy shape that you can do so without much trouble.

Choosing Your Size

This garment will look best if it's your bust width plus 2 to 4"/5 to 10 cm of ease. If you have a great disparity between your hips and bust—more than 6"/15.2cm—choose the size that suits your bust width. If you were to choose your hip width plus ease, it will look too baggy. When you sew the side seams of the sweater, leave about 4"/10.2cm of the bottom of the seam open, which will give you more wiggle room, literally.

> ## note
> *When making a sweater in two pieces, front and back, all the width measurements represent half the body width, including ease.*

LESSON 1: Altering Body and Sleeve Lengths

The body length should be determined by your overall proportions. For a top-heavy person with narrow hips, have the bottom hit right at your narrowest hip area. For a bottom-heavy person with wide hips or thighs, make it shorter to avoid calling attention to your widest part.

The measurement that's important is the total length figure, which ranges from 21"/53.3cm to 24"/61cm. Compare this to the measurement you took from your shoulder to various points on the hip. Where will this garment, as designed, land on your body? Is it at the high hip, low hip, or somewhere in between? Is this the hemline that's most flattering to your body? Will it accentuate you in the right spot?

The simplest way to add length is to work an extra pattern repeat—10 rows at the start of the sweater. From our gauge, we know this will add 3½"/8.9cm to the length. Where the pattern says work rows 2–11 four times, you will work those rows five times. Similarly, if you want the length shorter, you will work those rows three times and end up with a length that is 3½"/8.9cm shorter. Shortening is a good strategy if you are making a large size but are short in stature.

Suppose you want a length that doesn't fall neatly into this 3½"/8.9cm parameter. If you look at the stitch pattern, a natural dividing point occurs halfway through. You can begin the garment at row 6, resulting in five rows difference in length, adding or subtracting 1¾"/4.4cm as desired.

SLEEVE LENGTH

You'll notice that the length of the sleeves in this schematic decrease as the size gets larger. Oddly, that does not mean that the sleeve will actually be shorter for larger sizes. How low the sleeve hangs on the arm depends on your shoulder width. You can count on anywhere from 2"/5cm to 8"/20.3cm of fabric added to the given sleeve measurement. For the precise measure, refer to your wingspan measurement, discussed on page 21.

This design is meant to have the sleeves hit 1"/2.5cm or so below the elbow. If you haven't taken this elbow-to-elbow measurement, please do so. You want this measurement, plus 2"/5cm, to match the number at the very top of the schematic—the total width from one sleeve edge to the other.

If you are making the Large size, the pattern will give you a total wingspan, from just below one elbow to the other, of 48"/120cm.

Suppose this measurement is smaller on you, closer to 46"/115cm. At the sleeve, instead of having 6 pattern repeats, make 5. Since each pattern repeat is 2"/5cm long, this will give you the correct measurement. When you add the extra chains for the sleeves, the number will be 62 chains instead of 74.

For any size, if you find that the sleeve is too long or short, adjust it by removing, or adding, 1 or 2 pattern repeats from the sleeve length. For each pattern repeat more (or less), add (or subtract) 12 chains from the number given in the pattern at the start of the Sleeve section.

If you'd like to have the sleeve reach all the way to the wrist, figure out the difference by comparing your total wingspan from one wrist to the other and subtracting the width number at the top of the pattern.

For example, if your total wingspan to wrist is 54"/135cm and the pattern's wingspan is 48"/120cm, a difference of 6"/15.2cm, you need 3"/17.6cm more on each sleeve. Since each pattern repeat adds 2"/5cm, you'll have to decide whether you want the sleeve 1"/2.5cm shorter or longer than your wingspan (not a major decision, trust me!). Depending on your choice, you'll add one or two pattern repeats on each sleeve. When beginning your sleeves, add 12 chains to the number given in the pattern for each additional pattern repeat.

DOUBLE TROUBLE SHELL
modified rectangle construction

Here's a fashion-forward top based on motifs that are enhanced by filet work at the sides, shoulders, and neckline. And it's reversible—either side can be the front.

Motifs

Side A (Fan Side)

FIRST FAN MOTIF:

Ch 5, sl st to beg ch to form ring, or use magic loop.

RND 1: Ch 3 (counts as first dc), dc in ring, ch 2, *2 dc in ring, ch 2, rep from * 6 times, join with sl st in 3rd ch of beg ch-3—8 ch-2 sps.

RND 2: Ch 1, sc in next ch-2 sp, *ch 10, sc in same sp, (ch 5, sc) in next 2 ch-2 sps, rep from * twice, ch 10, sc in same sp, ch 5, sc in next ch-2 sp, ch 2, dc in top of beg sc instead of last ch-5 sp—4 ch-10 sps; 8 ch-5 sps.

RND 3: Ch 1, sc around the post of dc just made, *14 dc in next ch-10 sp, sc in next ch-5 sp, ch 5, sc in next ch-5 sp, rep from * twice, 14 dc in last ch-10 sp, sc in ch-5 sp, ch 2, dc in top of beg sc instead of last ch-5 sp—4 groups of 14 dc.

RND 4: Ch 1, sc around the post of dc just made, *sk next dc, (dc, ch 1) in next 5 dc, dc in next dc, ch 4, (dc, ch 1) in next 5 dc, dc in next dc, sk next dc**, (sc, ch 6, sc) in next ch-5 sp, rep from * twice, rep from * to ** once, sc in next ch-5 sp, ch 6, sl st in top of beg sc. Fasten off.

Make and join 19 more Fan Motifs, joining in a rectangle, 4 motifs wide by 5 motifs deep, as follows:

Side B (Square Side)

FIRST SQUARE MOTIF:

Ch 5, join with sl st to form ring, or use magic loop.

RND 1: Ch 1, 12 sc in ring, join with sl st to top of beg sc.

RND 2: Ch 1, sc in first sc *ch 7, sk next 2 sc, sc in next sc, rep from * twice, ch 7, join with sl st in top of beg sc.

RND 3: Sl st in next ch-7 sp, ch 3, 8 dc in ch-7 sp, ch 3, *9 dc in next ch-7 sp, ch 3, rep form * twice, join with sl st in top of beg ch-3.

RND 4: Ch 3, dc2tog over next 2 dc, *[ch 3, starting in same st as last dc, dc3tog over 3 dc] 3 times, ch 6, tr in next ch-3 sp, ch 6**, dc3tog over next 3 dc, rep from * twice, rep from * to ** once, join with sl st to 3rd ch of beg ch-3.

RND 5: Sl st in next ch-3 sp, ch 1, 3 sc in same sp, 3 sc in next 2 ch-3 sps, *ch 2, 3 sc in ch-6 sp, ch 3, 3 sc in next ch-6 sp, ch 2**, 3 sc in next 3 ch-3 sps, rep from * twice, rep from * to ** once, sl st in top of beg sc.

RND 6: Ch 1, sc in first sc, sc in next 8 sc, *2 sc in next ch-2 sp, sc in next 3 sc, (sc, ch 3, sc) in ch-3 corner sp, sc next 3 sc, 2 sc in next ch-2 sp**, sc next 9 sc, rep from * twice, rep from * to ** once, join with sl st to top of beg sc. Fasten off.

Make and join 19 more Fan Motifs, joining in a rectangle, 4 motifs wide by 5 motifs deep, as follows:

JOINING FAN MOTIFS ON ONE SIDE:

Work same as first Fan motif through Rnd 3.

RND 4: Ch 1, sc around the post of dc just made, *sk next dc, (dc, ch 1) in next 5 dc, dc in next dc, ch 4, (dc, ch 1) in next 5 dc, dc in next dc, sk next dc**, (sc, ch 6, sc) in next ch-5 sp, rep from * once, sk next dc, (dc, ch 1) in next 5 dc, dc in next dc, ch 2, sc in ch-4 sp of other motif, ch 2 (two corners joined), (dc, ch 1) in next 2 dc, dc in next dc, sc in third ch-1 sp of other motif, ch 1, (dc, ch 1) in next 2 dc, dc in next dc, sc in next ch-5 sp, ch 3, sc in ch-6 sp of other motif, ch 3, sc in same ch-5 sp, sk next dc, (dc, ch 1) in next 2 dc, dc in next dc, sc in third ch-1 sp of other motif, ch 1, (dc, ch 1) in next 2 dc, dc in next dc, ch 2, sc in ch-4 sp of other motif, ch 2 (two corners joined), rep from * to ** once, sc in next ch-5 sp, ch 6, sl st in top of beg sc. Fasten off.

FINISHED MEASUREMENTS

Bust 33 (38, 43)"/84 (96.5, 109)cm

MATERIALS AND TOOLS

Done Roving Farm Yarns Wrap it Up (100% bamboo rayon; 3 oz/85g = 300yd/270m): 2 (2, 3) skeins, color Poppy—approx 600 (600, 900)yds/540 (540, 810)m of fingering weight yarn; **①**

Crochet hook: 2.75mm (size C-2 U.S.)

Yarn needle

GAUGE

Each motif = 3"/7.6cm square before blocking; 3½"/8.9cm square blocked

Gauge for filet section: 4 rows (alternating 1 tr row and 1 sc row) = 1¼"/32mm; 28 sts = 4"/10.2cm

Always take time to check your gauge.

Special Abbreviations

dc2tog: [Yo, insert hook in next st, yo and draw up a loop, yo, draw yarn through 2 loops] twice, yo, draw yarn through 4 loops.

dc3tog: [Yo, insert hook in next st, yo and draw up a loop, yo, draw yarn through 2 loops] 3 times, yo, draw yarn through 4 loops.

tr2tog: [Yo (twice), insert hook in next designated st, yo and draw up a loop, (yo, draw yarn through 2 loops) twice] twice, yo, draw yarn through 3 loops.

tr3tog: [Yo (twice), insert hook in next designated st, yo and draw up a loop, (yo, draw yarn through 2 loops) twice] 3 times, yo, draw yarn through 4 loops.

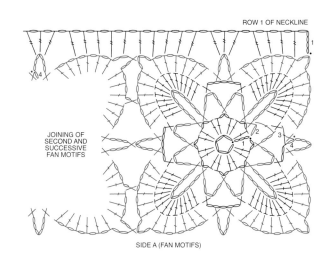

ROW 1 OF NECKLINE

JOINING OF
SECOND AND
SUCCESSIVE
FAN MOTIFS

SIDE A (FAN MOTIFS)

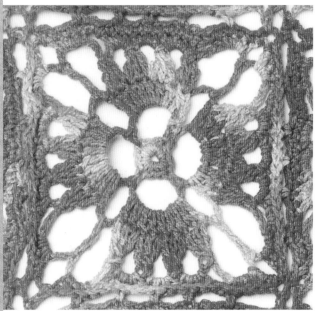

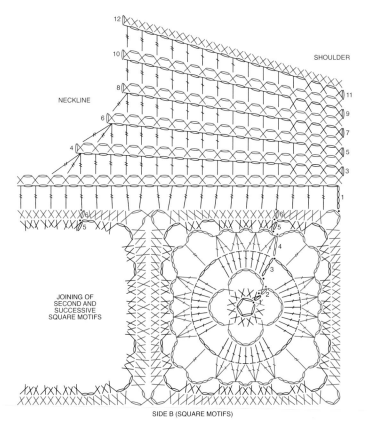

SHOULDER

NECKLINE

JOINING OF
SECOND AND
SUCCESSIVE
SQUARE MOTIFS

SIDE B (SQUARE MOTIFS)

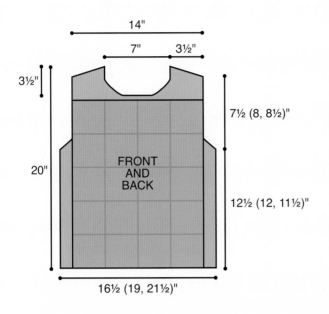

14"

7" 3½"

3½"

7½ (8, 8½)"

20"

FRONT
AND
BACK

12½ (12, 11½)"

16½ (19, 21½)"

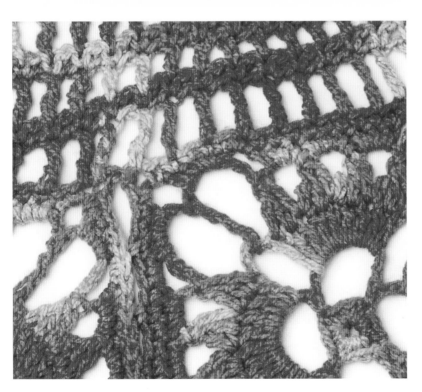

JOINING FAN MOTIFS ON TWO SIDES:
Work same as first Fan motif through Rnd 3.

RND 4: Ch 1, sc around the post of dc just made, *sk next dc, (dc, ch 1) in next 5 dc, dc in next dc, ch 4, (dc, ch 1) in next 5 dc, dc in next dc, sk next dc*, (sc, ch 6, sc) in next ch-5 sp, sk next dc, (dc, ch 1) in next 5 dc, dc in next dc, ch 2, sc in ch-4 sp of other motif, ch 2 (two corners joined), (dc, ch 1) in next 2 dc, dc in next dc, sc in third ch-1 sp of other motif, ch 1, (dc, ch 1) in next 2 dc, dc in next dc, sc in next ch-5 sp, ch 3, sc in ch-6 sp of other motif, ch 3, sc in same ch-5 sp, sk next dc, (dc, ch 1) in next 2 dc, dc in next dc, sc in third ch-1 sp of other motif, ch 1, (dc, ch 1) in next 2 dc, dc in next dc, ch 2, sc in ch-4 sp of other motif or in junction bet motifs, ch 2 (two corners joined)] twice, rep from * to * once, sc in next ch-5 sp, ch 6, sl st in top of beg sc. Fasten off.

JOINING SQUARE MOTIFS ON ONE SIDE:
Work same as first Square motif through Rnd 5.

RND 6: Ch 1, sc in first sc, sc in next 8 sc, *2 sc in next ch-2 sp, sc in next 3 sc, (sc, ch 3, sc) in ch-3 corner sp, sc next 3 sc, 2 sc in next ch-2 sp**, sc next 9 sts, rep from * once, (sc, ch 1, sc in corner sp of other motif, ch 1, sc) in next ch-3 corner sp, sc in next 2 sc, sc in next sc of both motifs, 2 sc in next ch-2 sp, sc in next sc, sc in next sc through both motifs, sc in next 2 sc, sc in next st through both motifs, sc in next 2 sc, sc in next sc of both motifs, sc in next sc, 2 sc in next ch-2 sp, sc in next sc of both motifs, sc in next 2 sts, (sc, ch 1, sc in corner sp of other motif, ch 1, sc) in ch-3 corner sp, sc next 3 sc, 2 sc in next ch-2 sp, join with sl st to beg sc.

JOINING SQUARE MOTIFS ON TWO SIDES:
Work same as first Square motif through Rnd 5.
RND 6: Ch 1, sc in first sc, sc in next 8 sts, 2 sc in next ch-2 sp, sc in next 3 sc, (sc, ch 3, sc) in ch-3 corner sp, sc next 3 sc, 2 sc in next ch-2 sp, sc next 9 sc, (sc, ch 1, sc in corner sp of other motif, ch 1, sc) in next ch-3 corner sp, *sc in next 2 sc, sc in next sc of both motifs, 2 sc in next ch-2 sp, sc in next st, sc in next sc through both motifs, sc in next 2 sc, sc in next sc through both motifs, sc in next 2 sc, sc in next sc of both motifs, sc in next sc, 2 sc in next ch-2 sp, sc in next sc of both motifs, sc in next 2 sc*, (sc, ch 1, sc in corner sp of adjacent motif, ch 1, skip diagonal corner of second motif, sc in corner space of third motif, ch 1, sc) in corner sp, rep from * to * once, (sc, ch 1, sc in corner sp of other motif, ch 1, sc) in corner sp sc next 3 sc, 2 sc in next ch-2 sp, join with sl st to beg sc.
Note: Longer edges of the rectangles are the sides of the body, shorter edges are across the top and bottom.

Neckline Across Side B (Square Motifs)

Note: After joining the motifs, work across the top to create the neckline. There will be 13 tr across each motif.

With RS facing, join yarn in top right-hand corner ch-3 sp of Side B rectangle.
ROW 1: Ch 5 (counts as tr, ch 1), *[tr in next sc, ch 1, sk next sc] 10 times, tr in next sc, ch 1, tr in next corner sp**, ch 1, tr in next corner sp, rep from * across top edge, ending last rep at **, turn—103 sts; 51 ch-1 sps.
ROW 2: Ch 1, sc in first tr, *ch 1, skip next ch-1 sp, sc in next tr, rep from * across, ending with last sc in 4th ch of tch, turn—103 sts; 51 ch-1 sps.

Left Shoulder Shaping

(See side B diagram on page 56)
ROW 3: Ch 1, sc in first sc, [ch 1, sk next ch-1 sp, sc in next st] 3 times, [ch 1, sk next ch-1 sp, hdc in next st] 5 times, [ch 1, sk next ch-1 sp, dc in next st] 4 times, [ch 1, sk next ch-1 sp, tr in next st] 3 times, ch 1, sk next ch-1 sp, tr3tog over next 3 sc, turn, leaving rem sts unworked—35 sts.

ROWS 4, 6, 8 AND 10: Ch 1, sc in first st, *ch 1, skip next ch-1 sp, sc in next st, rep from * across, ending with last sc in last sc, turn.
ROW 5: Ch 1, sc in first st, [ch 1, sk next ch-1 sp, sc in next st] twice, [ch 1, sk next ch-1 sp, hdc in next st] 5 times, [ch 1, sk next ch-1 sp, dc in next st] 4 times, [ch 1, sk next ch-1 sp, tr in next st] 3 times, ch 1, sk next ch-1 sp, tr3tog over next 3 sc, turn—2 sts.
ROW 7: Ch 1, sc in first st, [ch 1, sk next ch-1 sp, sc in next st] 3 times, [ch 1, sk next ch-1 sp, hdc in next st] 4 times, [ch 1, sk next ch-1 sp, dc in next st] 4 times, [ch 1, sk next ch-1 sp, tr in next st] twice, ch 1, sk next ch-1 sp, tr2tog over next 2 sc, turn—29 sts.
ROW 9: Ch 1, sc in first st, [ch 1, sk next ch-1 sp, sc in next st] 3 times, [ch 1, sk next ch-1 sp, hdc in next st] 4 times, [ch 1, sk next ch-1 sp, dc in next st] 4 times, [ch 1, sk next ch-1 sp, tr in next st] 3 times, turn—29 sts.
ROW 11: Ch 1, sc in first sc, [ch 1, sk next ch-1 sp, sc in next st] twice, [ch 1, sk next ch-1 sp, hdc in next st] 4 times, [ch 1, sk next ch-1 sp, dc in next st] 4 times, [ch 1, sk next ch-1 sp, tr in next st] 4 times, turn—29 sts.
ROW 12: Ch 1, sc in each st and in each ch-1 sp across (59 sc). Fasten off.

Right Shoulder Shaping

On opposite shoulder, with RS facing, join yarn in 39th st from left edge.
ROW 1 (REVERSE OF ROW 3 ON OPPOSITE SHOULDER): Ch 4, tr2tog over next 2 sc (counts as tr3tog), [ch 1, sk next ch-1 sp, tr in next sc] 4 times, [ch 1, sk next ch-1 sp, dc in next sc] 4 times, [ch 1, sk next ch-1 sp, hdc in next sc] 5 times, [ch 1, sk next ch-1 sp, sc in next sc] 4 times, turn—35 sts.
ROWS 2, 4, 6, AND 8: Ch 1, sc in first st, *ch 1, skip next ch-1 sp, sc in next st, rep from * across, ending with last sc in top of tch, turn.
ROW 3: Ch 4, tr2tog over next 2 sc (counts as tr3tog), [ch 1, sk next ch-1 sp, tr in next sc] 3 times, [ch 1, sk next ch-1 sp, dc in next sc] 4 times, [ch 1, sk next ch-1 sp, hdc in next sc] 5 times, [ch 1, sk next ch-1 sp, sc in next sc] 3 times, turn—31 sts.

ROW 5: Ch 4, tr in next sc (counts as tr2tog), [ch 1, sk next ch-1 sp, tr in next sc] twice, [ch 1, sk next ch-1 sp, dc in next sc] 4 times, [ch 1, sk next ch-1 sp, hdc in next sc] 4 times, [ch 1, sk next ch-1 sp, sc in next sc] 4 times, turn—29 sts.

ROW 7: Ch 5 (counts as tr, ch 1), sk next ch-1 sp, tr in next st, ch 1, sk next ch-1 sp, tr in next sc, [ch 1, sk next ch-1 sp, dc in next sc] 4 times, [ch 1, sk next ch-1 sp, hdc in next sc] 4 times, [ch 1, sk next ch-1 sp, sc in next sc] 4 times, turn—29 sts.

ROW 9: Ch 5 (counts as tr, ch 1), sk next ch-1 sp, tr in next st, [ch 1, sk next ch-1 sp, tr in next sc] twice, [ch 1, sk next ch-1 sp, dc in next sc] 4 times, [ch 1, sk next ch-1 sp, hdc in next sc] 4 times, [ch 1, sk next ch-1 sp, sc in next sc] 3 times, turn—29 sts.

ROW 10: Ch 1, sc in each st and in each ch-1 sp across (59 sc). Fasten off.

Neckline Across Side A (Fan Motifs)

(See side A diagram on page 56)
Note: There will be 13 tr across each motif.

With RS facing, join yarn in top right-hand corner ch-4 sp of rectangle.

ROW 1: Ch 5 (counts as tr, ch 1), *(tr, ch 1) in next 4 dc, sk next 2 dc, (tr, ch 1, tr, ch 1, tr, ch 1) in next ch-5 sp, sk next 2 dc, (tr, ch 1) in next 4 dc, tr in next ch-3 corner sp**, ch 1, tr in next ch-3 corner sp of next motif, ch 1 rep from * across, ending last rep at **, turn—103 sts; 51 ch-1 sps.

ROW 2: Ch 1, sc in first tr, *ch 1, skip next ch-1 sp, sc in next tr, rep from * across, ending with last sc in 4th ch of tch, turn—103 sts; 51 ch-1 sps.

Work shoulders same as on Side B.

Side Panels

PM 6½"/16.5cm below top of shoulder on left and right edges of both pieces.

SIDE B RIGHT SIDE PANEL:

With RS facing, join yarn in bottom right-hand corner ch-3 sp of Side B.

ROW 1: Ch 5 (counts as tr, ch 1 here and throughout), *[tr in next sc, ch 1, sk next sc] 10 times, tr in next sc, ch 1, tr in next corner sp, ch 1, tr in next corner sp, rep from * across to 6 sts before marker, sk next st, tr3tog over first, 3rd and 5th sc of next 5 sc group, turn.

ROW 2: Ch 1, sc in first tr, *ch 1, sk next ch-1 sp, sc in next tr, rep from * across, ending with last sc in 4th ch of tch, turn.

ROW 3: Ch 5, *sk next ch-1 sp, tr in next sc, ch 1, rep from * to last 3 sc, tr3tog over next 3 sc.

ROW 4: Rep Row 2. Fasten off size S only.

Sizes M and L only:
ROWS 5–8 (5–12): Rep Rows 3 and 4—once (twice). Fasten off.

SIDE B LEFT SIDE PANEL:

On opposite side of square panel, with RS facing, join yarn in marked st.

ROW 1: Ch 4, sk first 2 sc, tr2tog over first and 3rd sc of next 3 sc, *ch 1, sk next sc, tr in next sc, rep from * across, working 1 tr in each ch-3 corner sp, ending with tr in bottom corner ch-3 sp, turn.

ROW 2: Ch 1, sc in first tr, *ch 1, sk next ch-1 sp, sc in next tr, rep from * across.

ROW 3: Ch 4, tr2tog over next 2 st (counts as tr3tog), *ch 1, sk next ch-1 sp, tr in next sc, rep from * across, turn.

ROW 4: Rep Row 2. Fasten off size S only.

Sizes M and L only:
ROWS 5–8 (5–12): Rep rows 3 and 4—once (twice). Fasten off.

SIDE A RIGHT SIDE PANEL:

With RS facing, join yarn in bottom right-hand corner ch-4 sp of Side A.

ROW 1: Ch 5 (counts as tr, ch 1), *(tr, ch 1) in next 4 dc, sk next 2 dc, (tr, ch 1, tr, ch 1, tr, ch 1) in next ch-5 sp, sk next 2 dc, (tr, ch 1) in next 4 dc, tr in next ch-3 corner sp, ch 1, tr in next ch-3 corner sp of next motif, ch 1 rep from * across, ending 6 sts before marker, sk next st, tr3tog over first, 3rd and 5th st of next 5 sc group, turn.

Complete same as Side B right side panel.

SIDE A LEFT SIDE PANEL:

On opposite side of square panel, with RS facing, join yarn in marked st.

ROW 1: Ch 4, maintaining position of sts same as on right side panel, tr2tog over next 2 sts, work in patt across, ending with tr in bottom corner ch-4 sp, turn.

Complete same as side B left side panel.

Finishing

With RS of Sides A and B facing, work a sl st seam across sides, working in back lps only of sts. On one side, you will work from bottom to top, on the other from top to bottom. Work slowly and carefully to be sure that you are in the same place on both pieces. Working RS of Sides A and B, work sl st shoulder seams in same manner.

I'VE LONG WANTED to design a contemporary garment based on a rectangular panel of motifs that doesn't bring to mind doilies or bedspreads. This beautifully-dyed yarn gives the Double Trouble Shell eye appeal and a modern look. I love the way the two different motifs used in this design interact with the color changes. As the fashion runway keeps reminding us, lace has great sex appeal.

Construction Details

The front and back pieces of this design are two rectangles made out of connected motifs. A different motif is used on the back and front, and either side can be worn as the front—a truly reversible garment! After completing the rectangles, fabric is added at the sides with openwork filet panels. Filet is also used to construct the shoulders and neckline. The filet work makes use of treble stitches, which are particularly malleable. The result is a shoulder girdle that can cover a range of shoulder sizes and look fitted.

Substituting Yarn

This should be made with a slinky, lace-weight yarn—something with a bamboo or rayon component rather than 100-percent cotton. It would also look lovely in a lace-weight wool. A solid color can be used, but if you choose a variegated yarn, I would recommend subtle color variations, so that the motif patterns are noticeable.

Don't make the stitches as tight as you would in thread work; if you're used to wrapping your thread twice around a finger, skip the second wrap so you can crochet more loosely. In a way, that's more suitable for garment making. Let the stitches breathe more. Remember that the motifs will be blocked and will gain about ½"/1.3cm or more.

LESSON 2: Fine-Shaping Necklines and Shoulder Slope

The neckline and shoulder yoke make a good lesson on fine shaping.

Notice how the slant formed by the decreasing treble stitches at the inside edges of the rows creates a rounded neckline. This technique takes advantage of the natural lines created by tall stitches, as well as their maneuverability—they can be made to create a sharper or gentler diagonal. Beginning at the bottom of the neckline, the inside edges have decreases of tr3tog for 2 rows, then there is 1 row with tr2tog at the edge, making a gentler slope, then 2 rows with a straight, non-decreasing edge. You can see from this photo how this shapes the neckline.

LESSON 3: Blocking to Your Measurements

If you want dimensions different from those in the schematic, this is the easiest alteration you'll ever encounter! Because this is an openwork pattern made with thin yarn, you can block it to just the dimensions you need. Just pick a measurement up to 2"/5cm larger than what's on the schematic and stretch the finished piece to that measurement. You can control the entire width or length of the piece and make adjustments to the shoulder width and neckline depth too. It's a great pattern for perfecting your blocking technique.

For size Small, wet-block the motif rectangles when they're done, before adding the shoulder yoke. For all other sizes, wet-block after you've added the shoulder yoke, but not the side panels. That's because the width of the shoulder yoke needs no further stretching to fit a size small, but the larger sizes may want another 1 to 2"/2.5 to 5cm of width across the shoulders.

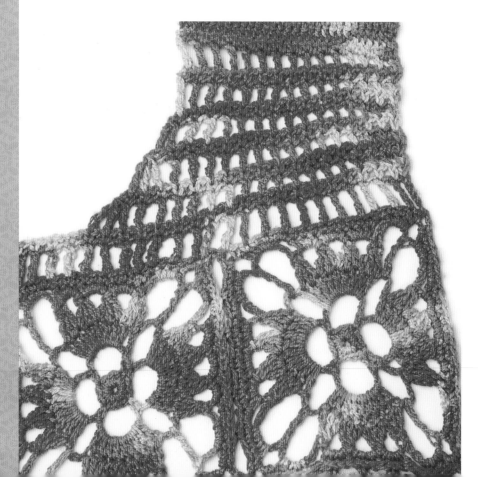

Here's how to pin your pieces to the blocking board effectively:

1. Start by pinning the entire outside edge, pulling it out to the required dimensions. Don't pin very closely yet, just at the corners and few other places so the piece will hold in place.

2. Adjust the motifs carefully in both directions (length and width) so they measure 3½"/8.9cm square. (You can make the motifs a little larger than that, but make sure they are still squares, measuring the same in length and width.) Once you've pulled them into place, pin along the outsides of the motifs to create well-shaped squares.

3. Pin the shoulder and neck section very carefully. While the schematic shows a neck depth of 3½"/8.9cm, this can be increased by blocking and creating more length between the top of the shoulder and the very bottom of the neckline.

4. The inside edge of the shoulder, next to the neck, should measure about 1½"/3.8cm more than the outside edge to account for shoulder slope. Be sure to pin the inside edge of each shoulder higher than the outside edge.

Additional Alteration Ideas

Lengthen the garment by adding edging or another row of motifs. If you are lengthening, remember it must be wide enough to cover your hips. Or, leave the bottom of the side seams open for a few inches/centimeters.

Drop the neckline by making additional rows worked even at the end of each shoulder. This will make the whole garment longer.

SHAWLED COLLAR TUNIC
vertical construction

This light-as-a-feather sweater is constructed vertically, which creates several alteration possibilities.

Stitch Pattern

Ch a multiple of 2 plus 1 + 1 for tch.

Row 1: (Sc, dc) in 2nd ch from hook, sk next ch, *(sc, dc) in next ch, sk next ch, rep from * across, sc in last ch, turn.

Row 2: Ch 1, (sc, dc) in first sc, sk next dc, *(sc, dc) in sc, sk next dc, rep from * across, sc in last sc, turn.

Rep row 2 for patt.

STITCH PATTERN

Special Notes

1. Work the foundation ch very loosely to make it the same length as the rest of the work. It should measure the length of garment when slightly stretched. If necessary, don't hesitate to use a larger hook for foundation chain only to achieve this length.

2. Every fourth row has 3 sts in the patt rep instead of 2, but only in the bottom portion. This is the Increase Row. It adds width to the garment from the hips down.

3. When working the row after the Increase Row, work the sc that stretches over two dc a bit looser than normal to minimize bulking up the larger st patt.

4. The individual rows can be hard to read in this stitch pattern. When you need to get a row count, hold the work so that you can see them running horizontally, and observe which way the stitches are slanting. In alternate rows, the stitches slant in the opposite direction, and this makes counting them much easier.

FINISHED MEASUREMENTS

Bust 36 (38, 41, 44, 48)"/91.4 (96.5, 104, 112, 122)cm

MATERIALS AND TOOLS

Louet KidLin (49% linen 35% kid mohair, 16% nylon, 1.75oz/50 g = 250yd/225m): 4 (4, 5, 5, 6) hanks, color 52 violet—approx 1000 (1000, 1250, 1250, 1500)yds/900 (1125, 1125, 1350, 1350)m of DK weight yarn; **3**

Crochet hook: 5mm (size H-8 U.S.)

Yarn needle

Snap for closure, 1/2"/13mm in diameter

Sewing needle

Matching sewing thread

Marker

GAUGE

3 patt reps = 2"/5cm; 10 rows in patt = 3"/7.6cm

Always take time to check your gauge.

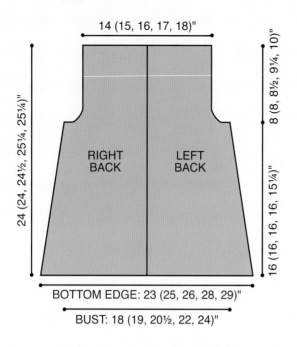

14 (15, 16, 17, 18)"

8 (8, 8½, 9¼, 10)"

RIGHT
BACK

LEFT
BACK

24 (24, 24½, 25¼, 25¼)"

16 (16, 16, 16, 15¼)"

BOTTOM EDGE: 23 (25, 26, 28, 29)"

BUST: 18 (19, 20½, 22, 24)"

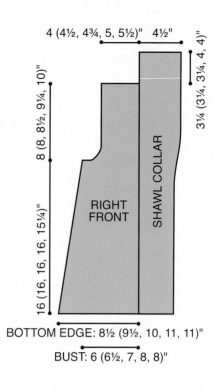

4 (4½, 4¾, 5, 5½)"   4½"

3¼ (3¼, 3¼, 4, 4)"

8 (8, 8½, 9¼, 10)"

RIGHT
FRONT

SHAWL COLLAR

16 (16, 16, 16, 15¼)"

BOTTOM EDGE: 8½ (9½, 10, 11, 11)"

BUST: 6 (6½, 7, 8, 8)"

Instructions

Left Back

Starting at center back, working in vertical rows, ch 74 (74, 76, 78, 78).)

ROWS 1–3: Work in patt across—36 (36, 37, 38, 38) patt reps. Mark beginning of Row 3 as top edge.

ROW 4 (INC ROW): Ch 1, (sc, 2 dc) in first sc (inc made), sk next dc, *(sc, 2 dc) in next sc, sk next ch, rep from * 10 times, PM, *(sc, dc) in next ch, sk next dc, rep from * across, sc in last sc, turn.

ROW 5: Work in patt to marker, *(sc, dc) in sc, sk next 2 dc, rep from * across, sc in last sc, turn.

ROWS 6 AND 7: Work even in patt.

ROWS 8 AND 9: Rep rows 4 and 5.

ROWS 10–21: Rep rows 6–9 (3 times).

ROWS 22–23 (25, 27, 28, 30): Work even in patt.

Note: Your piece should measure half the shoulder width at top.

Armhole Shaping

ROW 1: Ch 1, (sc, 2 dc) in first sc, sk next dc, *(sc, 2 dc) in next sc, sk next dc, rep from * 10 times, **sk next dc, (sc, dc) in next sc, rep from * 14 times, sk next dc, sc in next sc, turn, leaving rem sts unworked—26 patt reps.

ROW 2: Ch 1, sk first sc and next dc, (sc, dc) in next sc, sk next dc, work in patt to marker, *(sc, dc) in sc, sk next 2 dc, rep from * across, sc in last sc, turn—25 patt reps.

ROW 3: Work even in patt.

ROW 4: Rep row 2—24 patt reps.

ROWS 5 AND 6: Work even in patt.

Sizes S, M, and L only:

ROW 7: Work even in patt. Fasten off.

Sizes 1X and 2X only:

ROW 7: Rep row 2—23 patt reps.

ROWS 8 AND 9: Work even in patt. Fasten off size 1X only.

Size 2X only:

ROW 10: Work even in patt. Fasten off.

Right Back

Note: Check work carefully to find ch sts on foundation ch in which (sc, dc) are worked. You will work into these base ch sts.

With WS facing, working across opposite side of foundation ch, join yarn in first ch at top edge of Left Back.

ROW 1: Ch 1, (sc, dc) in first ch at base of st, sk next ch, *(sc, dc) in next ch at base of st, sk next ch, rep from * across to last ch, sc in last ch, turn.

Complete same as Left Back.

INC ROW ROW FOLL INC ROW

INCREASE PATTERN

Front (make 2)

Work same as right back through row 13 (15, 16, 15, 17).

Note: Piece should measure shoulder width at top edge.

Armhole Shaping

ROW 1: Ch 1, (sc, dc) in first sc, sk next dc, *(sc, dc) in next sc, sk next dc, rep from * 24 times, sc in next sc, turn, leaving rem sts unworked—26 patt reps.

ROW 2: Ch 1, sk next sc and dc, (sc, dc) in next sc, cont in patt across, turn—25 patt reps.

ROW 3: Ch 1, (sc, 2 dc) in first sc, sk next dc, *(sc, 2 dc) in next sc, sk next dc, rep from * 10 times, **(sc, dc) in next sc, sk next dc, rep from * across, sc in last sc, turn.

ROW 4: Rep row 2—24 patt reps.

ROWS 5 AND 6: Work even in patt. Fasten off.

Sizes S, M, and L only:

ROW 7: Work even in patt. Fasten off.

Sizes 1X and 2X only:

ROW 7: Rep row 2—23 patt reps.

ROWS 8 AND 9: Work even in patt. Fasten off size 1X only.

Size 2X only:

ROW 10: Work even in patt. Fasten off.

Shawl Collar

Note: This is added on to the starting foundation edge of the Left Front. Join yarn at top of foundation ch, ch 11 (11, 11, 13, 13), turn.

ROW 1: Ch 1, (sc, dc) in 2nd ch from hook, *(sc, dc) in next ch, sk next ch, rep from * 3 (3, 3, 4, 4) times, working across opposite side of foundation ch, **(sc, dc) in ch at base of next st, sk next ch, rep from * across, sc in last ch, turn—41 (41, 42, 42, 43) patt reps; (83, 83, 85, 85, 87) sts.

ROW 2: Ch 1, (sc, 2 dc) in first sc, sk next dc, *(sc, 2 dc) in next sc, sk next dc, rep from * 10 times, **(sc, dc) in next sc, sk next dc, rep from * across, sc in last sc, turn.

ROW 3: Work in patt to marker, *(sc, dc) in next sc, sk next 2 dc, rep from * across, sc in last sc, turn.

ROWS 4–5: Work even in patt.

ROWS 6–9: Rep rows 2–5.

ROW 10: Ch 1, sc in first 41 (41, 41, 39, 39) sts, beg regular patt in next sc, *(sc, dc) in sc, sk next 2 dc, rep from * across, sc in last sc, turn—41 (41, 41, 39, 39) sc plus 21 (21, 21, 23, 24) patt reps.

ROW 11: Work 21 (21, 21, 23, 24) patt reps, sk next sc, sc in each sc across, turn.

ROWS 12–16: Rep rows 10 and 11 (twice); then rep row 10 (once). Fasten off.

Finishing

Lightly steam pieces, especially at lower front edges, as the sc rows will tend to curl. This also smoothes out any bumps in fabric.

Sew side seams with mattress st on WS. To make a firm, strong seam for this fabric, sew shoulders with sl st seam on WS. Carefully pin collar in place, making sure center seam ends at center back, then sew in place with mattress st seam.

Repeat on the opposite Front piece. After you finish the second half of the Collar, continue sewing the two halves of the collar together.

Before sewing on snaps, this open mohair fabric needs to made more stable. First determine where the snaps will be placed by trying the garment on and marking the spot on Right Front. Measure from bottom of Left Front to place opposite side of snap. Place an 18"/45.5cm length of yarn on a tapestry needle and weave it in and out of a small area where the snap will be placed. This will make a more solid, stiff fabric to sew the snap onto. With sewing needle and sewing thread, sew the male side of snap on WS of Right Front; sew the female side on WS of Left Front (this will enhance the fold of the collar).

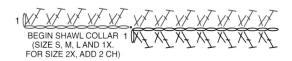

BEGIN SHAWL COLLAR
(SIZE S, M, L AND 1X.
FOR SIZE 2X, ADD 2 CH)

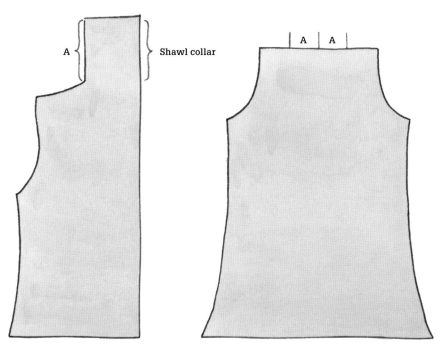

A is equal to the width of one-half of the back neck and will be attached to it.

VERTICAL CONSTRUCTION, sometimes called side-to-side construction, is particularly suited to crochet—where rows form prominent lines. We can turn this strong linear component of crochet on the vertical and make a garment with lines that are more flattering to the body. Vertical construction offers interesting shaping options, most notably widening the garment by making taller stitches. That strategy is exactly how the A-line shape is achieved in the Shawled Collar Tunic.

Construction Details

In most sweater constructions a collar is added to the neckline after it's done, but with vertical construction a collar can be built right on as you work. Termed a shawl collar, it grows out of the front lapels and then folds along the back of the neck. It's a very chic look, comfortable and functional, and easy to make.

Vertical construction can start either at the side seam of the garment, at the center, or at the edge of one sleeve, worked continuously across to the opposite sleeve. In this tunic, the back of the garment begins at the center and is worked out to the sides. We begin with the full length of the tunic and work enough rows for half of the desired shoulder width. After this point, we create the armhole. The second half of the back is made by building directly on to the starting foundation chain and working out to the opposite side. Note that the back along the top is completely flat. Because of the soft, malleable fabric, shoulder shaping is not necessary.

The front of the garment is in two pieces, with the shawl collar added. We begin the front pieces right outside the neckline, following the same directions as on the back, but with fewer rows. When that section is done, we tie on at the foundation edge, and add chains for the length of the shawl collar.

If you examine the illustration on the previous page you can see that the shawl collar extends in length from the shoulder of the front piece. The left side of that extension (indicated with a bracket) needs to be half the width of the back neck; it will be sewn to the back neck. On the opposite Front piece, the other half of the shawl collar will be sewn to the other half of the back neck, and then

the two halves of the shawl collar are sewn together at the center.

Making the collar at the end allows you to make it as wide as you like. Any extra rows added to the collar will make it wider.

Another detail to call to your attention to is how the rows for the collar are handled at the garment's bottom edge. To avoid having the entire front piece become as wide as the collar section, we change to single crochet stitches for the lower section of these rows. These smaller stitches create a denser fabric at the front edges. The rather wispy fabric can benefit from the stability of a denser fabric at the front edges and corners, allowing the garment to hang more neatly. Be sure to take full advantage of finishing techniques and block to keep the front edges from curling.

Substituting Yarn

The fabric of this garment is determined by its mohair content, which makes it soft, lightweight, and very fluid. If you use a different mohair yarn than the one used here, make sure it is not super fuzzy—the yarn weight should be DK weight or finer. If you are not going to work it in mohair, remember that drape and fluidity are important considerations for this garment to look its best. Choose a fiber with good drape, like silk or bamboo. With a different fiber than mohair, you will probably find you can match gauge with a DK weight and a large hook. As always, swatch first before you decide.

If substituting a different yarn, I also advise that you make a test run of the final rows on the front to see if the single crochet stitches will match in length with the rows of pattern stitches. The yarn used here has a natural stretch, but other yarns may behave differently.

Fit and Choosing Your Size

For a flattering fit, the garment should be close-fitting on the upper body; the shoulders should match your shoulder width or be slightly narrower, not wider. The bust width should also match, with the amount of ease you prefer. If your shoulder width matches one size and your bust width another (check the schematic!), follow the instructions for the

size that is appropriate for your shoulders until the pattern says "Armhole Shaping," then switch to the size that's appropriate to your bust width. The length should be adjusted to accommodate your height and body proportions. Do this on all sections of the vest, back and front.

The collar is relatively narrow. The larger sizes in this style may benefit from enlarging the width of the collar to make it more proportional to the garment. The neckline forms a pronounced, figure–flattering V shape. You can choose exactly where the base of that V is when placing the snaps that close the front.

LESSON 4: Altering Length

Changing the length of this design, with its simple pattern stitch, is easy. To calculate how many pattern repeats (PR) are needed, use the stated gauge, which is 3 PR = 2"/5cm. This means that for every 2"/5cm of difference in length, you should add or subtract 3 PR. Add these to row 1 of the pattern. When computing the number of starting chains, you will change the stitch count by 2 for each PR you are adding or subtracting.

Suppose you want to make the garment 3"/7.6cm shorter:

3"/7.6cm divided by 2"/5cm (the inch/cm number in our gauge equation) = 1.5

1.5 x 3 (the number of PR in our gauge equation) = 4.5

This tells me that an alteration exactly 3"/7.6cm in length would require 4 1/2 PR, so let's make either 4 (2 2/3"/6.8cm) or 5 (3 1/3"/8.5cm) PR. The alteration will be either a little more, or a little less, than 3"/7.6cm.

A-LINE SHAPING

However, if you are making a big change in length—more than 3"/7.6cm—I recommend you consider where to place the enlarged PR that create the A-line. This shaping should begin just under the waistline.

To adjust the A-line shaping, refer to your measurement from underarm to waist. Suppose the length from your underarm to waist is 7"/17.8cm. You want this A-line shaping to begin after it passes your waist and to extend to the bottom. Since the garment is now 13"/33cm long in this area instead of 16"/40.6cm, you will only need the enlarged PR for the bottom 6"/15.2cm.

Here's the math:

> 6"/15.2cm divided by the 2"/5cm side of the gauge equation = 3.

> Gauge tells us that for each 2"/5cm segment, you need 3 PR.

> 3 (2"/5cm segments) x 3 (PR per 2"/5cm segment) = 9 PR.

So instead of working 12 PR with enlarged PR as instructed in Row 4 of the pattern, you will do so on only 9, on the rows where enlarged PR are made. You will make this pattern with 4 or 5 PR less to begin with for your size.

To rewrite the instructions for the pattern, begin by looking at the number of PR for your size. Subtract either 4 or 5 PR from that total. Now adjust the number of starting chains: the total number of PR x 2, plus 1 more for the turning chain. The first 3 rows of the pattern will be the same except for the number of PR. The change comes on row 4, which is written:

Row 4 (inc row): Ch 1, (sc, 2 dc) in first sc (inc made), sk next dc, *(sc, 2 dc) in next sc, sk next ch, rep from * 10 times, PM, *(sc, dc) in next ch, sk next dc, rep from * across, sc in last sc, turn.

---

note

For all length adjustments, when working vertical rows, you must adjust the stitch or PR counts at the bottom of the garment. That way, the alteration will have no effect on the depth of the armhole.

For your alteration, after the asterisk in this row, you will repeat 8 times, giving you a total of 9 tall PR. You will also need to adjust the number of PR at the Armhole Shaping section. The first row of Armhole Shaping begins at the bottom and extends for 26 PR. In your shorter version, there are 4 or 5 PR fewer, so you will work 21 or 22 PR. This will preserve the armhole depth as written for your size.

If you were to add 3"/7.6cm in length, you would need to add those 4 or 5 PR at the very beginning of the pattern, adding the necessary number of extra chains when you start the sweater. You will also add them on to the number of PR in row 1 of the Armhole Shaping section.

LESSON 5: Widening the Collar

This alteration couldn't be simpler—just keep working additional rows at the front edges until you get to the desired width. Change to sc at the bottom of the row as is done on previous collar rows. You can also make this alteration after you have sewn the collar pieces together at the back, allowing you to see the collar width as-is, first. If you decide at that point to widen it, work continuously from the bottom of one front edge all the way around the back neck to the bottom of the other front piece.

IN VEST
fitted armhole and v-neck construction

A clean, modern take on a classic silhouette, In Vest presents lessons in waist shaping, bust line alteration, and fitted armholes.

Stitch Pattern

Ch a multiple of 6 plus 1 + 2 for tch.

Row 1: Dc in 4th ch from hook, dc in next 4 ch, *ch 1, sk next ch, dc in next 5 ch, rep from * across, dc in last ch, turn.

Row 2: Ch 1, sc in each st and ch-1 sp across, turn.

Row 3: Ch 2 (counts as hdc here and throughout), *dc/FPdc, dc in next 3 sc, FPdc/dc**, ch 1, sk next sc, rep from * across, ending last rep at **, hdc in last sc, turn.

Rep rows 2 and 3 for patt.

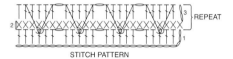

STITCH PATTERN

Instructions

Back
Ch 93 (105, 117, 129, 141)
ROWS 1–3: Work in patt on 15 (17, 19, 21, 23) patt reps—91 (103, 115, 127, 139) sts.

Hip to Waist Shaping
Note: 8 sts will be decreased over next 7 rows. Decreasing occurs in every other row.

ROWS 4-10: Maintaining patt as established, dec 1 sc at each end of Row 4 and every other row 3 times—83 (95, 107, 119, 131) sts at end of last row.
ROWS 11–15: Work even in patt.

Waist to Bust Shaping
ROW 16 (INC): Ch 1, 2 sc in first sc (inc made), sc in each st across to last st, 2 sc in top of tch (inc made), turn—85 (97, 109, 121, 133) sts.
ROW 17 (EVEN): Ch 2, dc in next 2 sc, work in patt across to last 4 sts, ch 1, sk next sc, dc in next 2 sc, hdc in last sc, turn.
ROWS 18–21: Work even in patt.
ROW 22: Rep Rows 16—87 (99, 111, 123, 135) sts.
ROWS 23–27: Work even in patt.
ROW 28: Rep Rows 16—89 (101, 113, 125, 137) sts.
ROWS 29–33: Work even in patt.
ROW 34: Rep Rows 16—91 (103, 115, 127, 139) sts.
ROWS 35–46: Work even in patt.

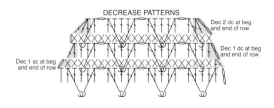

DECREASE PATTERNS

Dec 1 sc at beg and end of row

Dec 2 dc at beg and end of row

Dec 1 dc at beg and end of row

FINISHED MEASUREMENTS
Chest 32 (36, 40 1/2, 45, 49)"/81.5 (91.5, 103, 114.5, 124.5)cm

MATERIALS AND TOOLS
Skacel Zitron Lifestyle (100% merino superwash, 1.75oz/50g = 170 yd/153m): 4 (5, 5, 6, 6) skeins, color 12 silver—approx 680 (850, 850, 1020)yds /612 (765, 765, 918, 918)m of fingering weight yarn; (1)

Crochet hook: 3.5mm (size E-4 U.S.)

Stitch markers

Yarn needle

GAUGE
4 pattern repeats = 4 1/4"/10.8cm; 16 rows = 4"/10.2cm

Always take time to check your gauge.

Special Abbreviations

sc2tog: [insert hook in next st, yo and draw up a loop] twice, yo, draw yarn through 3 loops.

dc2tog: [yo, insert hook in next st, yo and draw up a loop, yo, draw yarn through 2 loops] twice, yo, draw yarn through 3 loops.

dc3tog: [yo, insert hook in next st, yo and draw up a loop, yo, draw yarn through 2 loops] 3 times, yo, draw yarn through 4 loops.

sc/FPdc: insert hook in next st and draw up a loop, yo, insert hook around the post of st 2 sts to the left and 2 rows below, yo, draw through 2 loops, yo, draw through 3 loops.

Continued on next page

FPdc/sc: Yo, insert hook around the post of st 2 sts to the right and 2 rows below, yo, draw through 2 loops, insert hook in next dc in current row, draw up a loop, yo, draw through 3 loops.

hdc/FPdc: yo, insert hook in next st and draw up a loop, yo, insert hook around the post of st 2 sts to the left and 2 rows below, draw up a loop, yo, draw yarn through 2 loops, yo, draw through 3 loops.

FPdc/hdc: yo, insert hook around the post of st 2 sts to the right and 2 rows below, draw up a loop, yo, draw through 2 loops, yo, insert hook in next dc in current row, draw up a loop, yo, draw through 3 loops.

dc/FPdc: yo, insert hook in next st and draw up a loop, yo, draw through 2 loops, yo, insert hook around the post of st 2 sts to the left and 2 rows below, draw up a loop, yo, draw yarn through 2 loops, yo, draw through 3 loops.

FPdc/dc: yo, insert hook around the post of st 2 sts to the right and 2 rows below, draw up a loop, yo, draw through 2 loops, yo, insert hook in next st in current row, draw up a loop, yo, draw yarn through 2 loops, yo, draw through 3 loops.

tr/FPtr: yo (twice), insert hook in next st and draw up a loop, [yo, draw through 2 loops] twice, yo (twice), insert hook around the post of st 2 sts to the left and 2 rows below, draw up a loop, [yo, draw yarn through 2 loops], yo, draw through 3 loops.

FPtr/tr: yo (twice), insert hook around the post of st 2 sts to the right and 2 rows below, draw up a loop, [yo, draw through 2 loops] twice, yo, insert hook in next st in current row, draw up a loop, [yo, draw yarn through 2 loops] twice, yo, draw through 3 loops.

Always ch 2 at start of dc rows, and make last st of dc rows an hdc (or tight dc). This will make end stitches the same height as other stitches, which are not as tall as usual because they are pulled in by crossed post stitches.

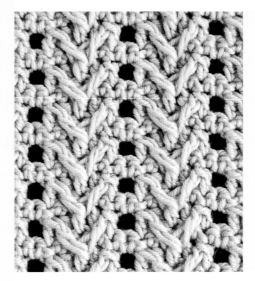

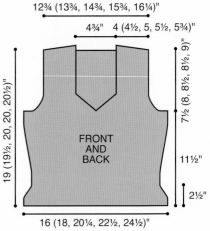

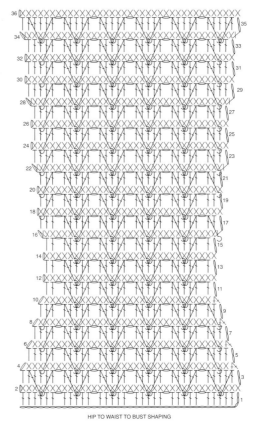

HIP TO WAIST TO BUST SHAPING

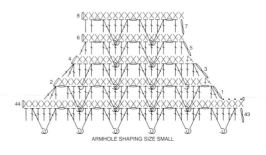

ARMHOLE SHAPING SIZE SMALL

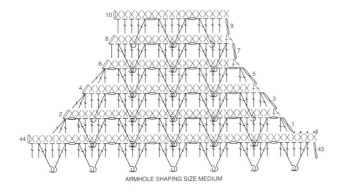

ARMHOLE SHAPING SIZE MEDIUM

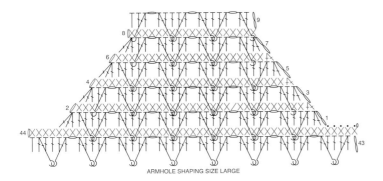

ARMHOLE SHAPING SIZE LARGE

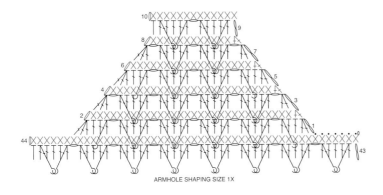

ARMHOLE SHAPING SIZE 1X

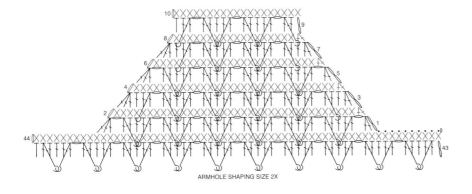

ARMHOLE SHAPING SIZE 2X

Armhole Shaping

Sizes S, M, and 2X only:

ROW 1: Ch 1, sl st over first 4 (4, 10) sts, ch 2, dc2tog in next 2 sts (counts as dc3tog here and throughout—dec 2 dc made), work in established patt across completing 13 (15, 19) patt reps, ch 1, sk next st, dc3tog in next 3 sts (dec 2 dc made), turn, leaving rem sts unworked—81 (93, 117) sts.

Size L only:

ROW 1: Ch 1, sl st over first 5 sts, ch 2, dc2tog (counts as dc3tog—dec 2 dc made), dc/FPdc in next st, dc in next 3 sts, FPdc/dc, work in patt across to last 7 sts, dc3tog in next 3 sts (dec 2 dc made), turn, leaving rem sts unworked—103 sts.

Size 1X only:

ROW 1: Ch 1, sl st over first 7 sts, ch 2, dc2tog (counts as dc3tog—dec 2 dc made), dc in next 2 sts, FPdc/dc, work in patt across to last 13 sts, dc/FPdc, dc in next 2 sts, dc3tog in next 3 sts (dec 2 dc made), turn, leaving rem sts unworked—111 sts.

All Sizes:

ROW 2: Maintaining patt as established, dec 1 sc at each end of row, turn—79 (91, 102, 109, 115) sts.

ROW 3: Maintaining patt as established, dec 2 dc at each end of row, turn—75 (87, 98, 105, 111) sts.

ROW 4: Maintaining patt as established, dec 1 sc at each end of row, turn—73 (85, 96, 101, 109) sts.

In Vest **73**

Size S only:

ROW 5: Maintaining patt as established, dec 1 dc at each end of row, turn—71 sts.

Sizes M, L, 1X, and 2X only:

ROW 5: Maintaining patt as established, dec 2 dc at each end of row, turn—81 (92, 97, 105) sts.

ROW 6: Maintaining patt as established, dec 1 sc at each end of row, turn—79 (90, 95, 103) sts.

Size M only:

ROW 7: Maintaining patt as established, work even.

ROW 8: Maintaining patt as established, dec 1 sc at each end of row, turn—77 sts.

Sizes L, 1X, and 2X only:

ROW 7: Maintaining patt as established, dec 2 dc at each end of row, turn—86 (91, 99) sts.

Sizes 1X and 2X only:

ROW 8: Maintaining patt as established, dec 1 sc at each end of row, turn—77 sts.

All Sizes:

Work even in patt until 30 (32, 34, 34, 36) rows are complete from beg of armhole shaping, ending with a sc row.

Right Shoulder Shaping

Size S only:

ROW 1: Ch 1, sc in first sc, sc in next sc, ch 1, sk next st, sc/FPdc, sc in next sc, hdc in next 2 sc, FPdc/hdc, ch 1, sk next st, hdc/FPdc, hdc in next sc, dc in next 2 sc, FPdc/dc in next sc, ch 1, sk next st, dc/FPdc, dc in next sc, tr in next 2 sc, FPtr/tr in next sc, ch 1, sk next st, tr in next sc, turn—22 sts.

Sizes M, L, 1X, and 2X only:

ROW 1: Ch 1, sc in first 4 (2, 5, 2) sc, FPdc/sc, ch 1, sk next st, hdc/FPdc, hdc in next 3 sc, FPdc/hdc in next sc, ch 1, sk next st, dc/FPdc in next sc, dc in next 3 sc, FPdc/dc in next sc, ch 1, sk next st, [tr/FPtr in next sc, tr in next 3 sc, FPtr/tr in next sc, ch 1, sk next st] 1 (2, 1, 2) times, tr in next 1 (1, 5, 4) sc, turn—26 (29, 30, 32) sts. Fasten off.

Left Shoulder Shaping

Size S only:

ROW 1: With RS facing, skip next 27 sts to the left of last st made in Row 1 of right shoulder, join yarn In next st, ch 5 (counts as tr, ch 1), sk next st, tr/FPtr, tr in next 2 sts, dc in next st, FPdc/dc, ch 1, sk next st, dc/FPdc, dc in next 2 sts, hdc in next st, FPdc/hdc, ch 1, sk next st, hdc/FPdc, hdc in next 2 sts, sc in next st, FPdc/sc, ch 1, sk next st, sc in last 2 sts, turn—22 sts.

ROW 2: Ch 1, sc in each st and sp across. Fasten off.

Sizes M, L, 1X, and 2X only:

ROW 1: With RS facing, skip next 27 (27, 33, 33) sts to the left of last st made in Row 1 of right shoulder, join yarn In next st, ch 5 (5, 4, 4), sk next 1 (1, 0, 0) st, tr in next 0 (0, 4, 3) sts, ch 1, sk next st, [tr/FPtr, tr in next 3 sts, FPtr/tr, ch 1, sk next st] 1 (2, 1, 2) times, dc/FPdc, dc in next 3 sts, FPdc/dc, ch 1, sk next st, hdc/FPdc, hdc in next 3 sts, FPdc/hdc, ch 1, sk next st, sc/FPdc, sc in next 4 (2, 5, 2) sts, turn—26 (29, 30, 32) sts.

ROW 2: Ch 1, sc in each st and sp across. Fasten off.

Front

Work same as back to armhole shaping.

Left Front

At the beginning of all RS rows you are working the armhole, at the end of the row the V-neck. On all WS rows, the beginning of the row is V-neck shaping, the end of the row is armhole. Place a marker in center st of last row.

ROW 1: Ch 1, sl st over first 4 (4, 5, 7, 10) sts, ch 2, dc2tog in next 2 sts, maintaining patt same as back, work across to 4 sts of marked center st (completing 6 (7, 8, 9, 9) patt reps), ch-1, sk next st, dc3tog in next 3 sts, ending in marked center st, turn, leaving rem sts unworked—39 (45, 50, 53, 57) sts.

ROW 2: Ch 1, sk first dc, sc in each st and sp across to last 2 sts, sc2tog in last 2 sts—37 (43, 48, 51, 56) sts.

Work armhole shaping on RS same as back, at the same time, work neck edge as follows: *dec 1 sc at beg of next WS row, dec 2 dc at end of next RS row, rep from * 3 (3, 3, 4, 4) times. Work even on 22 (25, 29, 29, 32) sts until 30 (32, 34, 34, 36) rows are complete from beg of armhole shaping, ending with a sc row.

Left Shoulder

ROWS 1 AND 2: Work same as Rows 1 and 2 of Back Right Shoulder Shaping. Fasten off.

Right Front

ROW 1: With RS facing, join yarn in center marked st in last row of before armhole shaping, already holding last st of Row 1 of left front, ch 2, dc2tog in next 2 sts, work in patt across to last 6 (6, 7, 9, 12) sts, dc3tog in next 3 sts, turn leaving rem sts unworked—37 (43, 48, 51, 56) sts.

Work armhole shaping on left side same as back, at the same time, work neck edge as follows: *dec 1 sc at end of next WS row; dec 2 dc at beg of next RS row, rep from * 3 (3, 3, 4, 4) times. Work even on 22 (25, 29, 29, 32) sts until 30 (32, 34, 34, 36) rows are complete from beg of armhole shaping, ending with a sc row.

Finishing

Block pieces to even out stitches and adjust all measurements. With RS facing, sew side seams. With RS facing, sc shoulder seams.

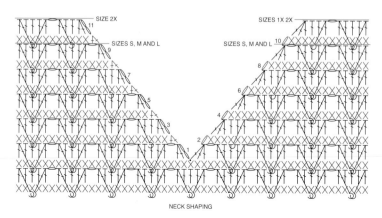

NECK SHAPING

IN VEST, A CLASSIC V-neck vest, uses a pretty dimensional stitch created from post stitches made at an angle. The bulk of these crossed stitches dictates that the vest should be made in a relatively fine-weight yarn. The shoulders are cut narrow. That element, plus the V-neck, will create a slimming effect. Sharply-angled waist shaping on this design accentuates the waistline.

Construction Details

The vest is worked in two pieces from the bottom up, tapering from hip to waist, then widening again between waist and bust. It has a fitted armhole. On the front, you will be shaping the armhole and the V-neck at the same time.

To simplify this pattern, you might want to work straight up from the bottom, ignoring the instructions for waist-shaping rows. Simply keep your stitch count the same from the beginning of the pattern up to the armhole and ignore all the shaping instructions, but work the same number of rows up to the armhole for your size. If you choose this option, pick a fiber with drape that will nicely do the shaping around your curves for you.

Substituting Yarn

The stitch pattern looks best with a high-definition fiber, such as merino or cotton. Tightly twisted yarns show more stitch definition than do those with a loose twist. Use fingering (or perhaps sport) weight yarn.

Fit and Choosing Your Size

The fit on this garment can be snug or more relaxed. Many elements can be altered, including the overall length, the depth of the V-neck, and the degree of waist shaping.

Find the size where the schematic measurement for the bust matches your bust width plus ease. Then check if the shoulder width and overall length are suitable. Remember that the finished shoulder width can be smaller by 1"/2.5cm (or so) than your actual shoulder width, as the design is cut narrow in the shoulder.

LESSON 6: Altering Length and Waist Placement

If you want to change the overall length of the vest, you will make this adjustment in the first portion of the sweater, by adding or subtracting rows before the armhole. You can also change the placement of the waist, making it higher or lower. Both of these alterations may require that you modify the shaping rows going from hip to waist and/or from waist to bust. Make sure you refer to the measurements of where your waistline lies in relation to your underarm and your high hip. The schematic tells you that underarm to hip measures 11½"/29.2cm, and that the waist occurs 2½"/6.4cm above the hip.

Let's use the techniques detailed in Shaping and Alteration 101 (Tapered Shaping, page 38) to plot out such an alteration, using a specific example. Suppose you are making the size Medium and want the vest to be longer, 13"/33cm instead of 11½"/29.2cm. Our length gauge is 16 rows = 4"/10.2cm, and some easy math tells you the extra 1½"/3.8cm will require 6 rows.

In this pattern, Rows 1 through 3 are worked even. The waist shaping begins on Row 4 and is completed after Row 10; but in your alteration you will add 6 rows, so the waist shaping will be complete on row 16 instead. To be sure the vest doesn't get tight over the hips, work the first 3 rows even as in the original pattern. Now you have 13 rows left for your waist shaping. You want to remove the same number of stitches (8) over these 13 rows. Notice that decreases only occur on single crochet rows. In the original, the decreases are made on rows 4, 6, 8, and 10, so there are 4 decrease rows. You've got 3 more sc rows to work with, for a total of 7 shaping rows.

Take half the number of stitches to be decreased, which is 4, and divide the number of decrease rows by the number of stitches—7 decrease rows divided by 4 = 1.75.

We can't make a fraction of a row, so round this up to 2. Every second single crochet row will be a decrease row, so your decreases will occur on rows 4, 8, 12, and 16.

If you wanted the waistline to be a bit higher than on the schematic, you could spread the decreases out even more. In the same way, the increases going from waist to bust can be spread out or compressed, depending on now many inches/cm you want between the waist and full bust width.

LESSON 7: Master Class in Fitted Armholes

A fitted armhole requires a decrease in the number of stitches between the bust and the shoulder. As mentioned before, the larger the size, the more stitches need to be removed between bust and shoulder. Based on the pattern shapes of woven garments, fitted armholes should look like the illustration below if they are to conform nicely to the body's curves. Fitted armholes have three sections:

Section 1 The initial bind-off, where about 1/2 to 2"/1.3 to 5cm of stitches are removed all at once. Note that a bind-off is a term borrowed from knitting, and it simply means that the stitches are removed all at once. In crochet, at the beginning of the row it will usually be done with slip stitches, while at the end of the row the unwanted stitches will be skipped.

Section 2 The next section of the armhole is tapered. After the bound-off stitches in the first section are subtracted from the stitch count, there will still be stitches left to decrease to get to shoulder width. These are usually removed at the rate of 1 or 2 stitches per row. Since there are more stitches to get rid of with larger sizes, there are usually more rows of decrease at the armhole as the size increases.

Section 3 The remainder of the armhole is worked straight, with no shaping, up to the shoulder. How many rows are in this section depends on the armhole depth. Both the tapering rows in Section 2 and the straight rows in this section contribute to armhole depth.

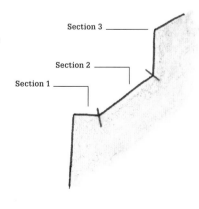

With this understanding of the fitted armhole, we can discuss how it can be altered. Two different alterations can be made on an armhole: It can change in length, which makes armhole depth longer or shorter, or it can be altered in width, which affects the shoulder width of the garment. Let's look at both.

ALTERING ARMHOLE DEPTH

Changing the length of an armhole is very useful alteration for people who are full at the bust but thin in the arms. Typically, a sweater that will correctly fit the bust on this kind of body will have an armhole depth that is too deep.

The adjustment will be only 1"/2.5cm or so. Look at the total number of rows in the pattern at the armhole, both the tapering rows and the straight rows. In this pattern that number is given where the pattern says:

All Sizes:
Work even in patt until 30 (32, 34, 34, 36) rows are complete from beg of armhole shaping, ending with a sc row.

Refer to the armhole depth you recorded in your measurements. Using row gauge (page 37), figure out how many rows to subtract. Subtract those rows in Section 3 of the armhole, that is, the top part, where the rows are worked straight. You will be changing its shape shown below.

Note that if you shorten the armhole depth, you will also have fewer rows for the neckline.

ALTERING SHOULDER WIDTH AT THE ARMHOLE

It's not uncommon to find a pattern fits you in most places but is off by 1"/2.5cm or so at the shoulder width. On a design with a fitted armhole, a shoulder width alteration must be done at the armhole. This is an important alteration for those whose shoulder width is small or large in relation to their bust size. If you pick the size appropriate to your bust width, you will have to decrease or increase more stitches than the pattern does to get to your proper shoulder width.

Check the pattern to find the stitch count for your size at the end of Section 2 of the armhole. You'll find it in the last row before the "All Sizes" instruction noted at left.

Let's look at a concrete example from this vest. If the bust size you're making has a 17"/43.2cm shoulder width, and you want it to be 15"/38.cm, you'll remove 2"/5cm altogether, 1"/2.5cm from the width of each armhole.

Here's the math:

The gauge is 4 PR (24 sts) = 4

1/4"/10.8cm. 2"/5cm divided by 4 1/4/10.8cm (the inch/cm number in your gauge equation) = 0.47

0.47 x 24 (the stitch number in gauge equation) = 11.28

This gives you the number of stitches to be removed. Since you need to shape on both sides of the garment, round up to an even number, 12. In Section 2 of the armhole,

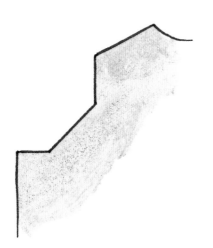

Armhole without alteration

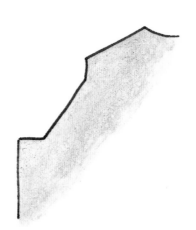

Shorter armhole

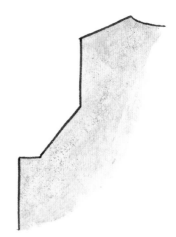

Taller (deeper) armhole

decrease 6 more stitches on each side of the garment. On this pattern decreases occur every row: 4 stitches are removed on the double crochet rows, 2 on the single crochet rows. That means you'll need 4 more rows— alternating double crochet and single crochet rows as you have throughout the pattern—to get to the correct width.

The 4 rows added here must be subtracted from Section 3 (the straight part of the armhole); otherwise you'll end up with a deeper armhole. So, for example, if this alteration is being made on size Large, there will be 11 rows of tapering in Section 2 of the armhole instead of 7. To maintain the correct total row count of 34 for the armhole, you will work 23 rows even. The armhole depth remains the same. To reiterate, altering the shoulder width is actually an alteration made at the armhole.

Let's summarize the steps involved, so they can be applied to different garments:

1. Check the schematic for your size, and determine how many inches/cm of difference between your shoulder width and the shoulder width on the pattern.

2. Use stitch gauge (page 37) to determine the difference between the number of stitches you need, and the number of stitches in the pattern. Divide that difference in half, since you will be shaping on both right and left armholes.

3. Check the stitch counts in Section 2, the tapered part of the armhole, to see how many stitches are removed at each decrease. If you continue decreasing at the same rate, determine how many additional rows you will need to arrive at the required number of stitches determined in step 2.

4. Once you've determined how many extra rows you need in Step 3, subtract that number of rows from Section 3 (the straight part of the armhole). This will keep the total number of rows at the armhole the same, so that your armhole depth does not change.

In general, decrease at the same rate as the pattern recommends, just to keep things simple. It is also possible to decrease more rapidly, by removing more stitches at each decrease. Alternatively, you can spread your decreases over more rows.

FIJI CARDI
fitted sleeve cardigan

A variation on the classic cardigan, Fiji has an intriguing stitch pattern that varies with the sizes and flows around the sweater.

Stitch Patterns

Size Small:
Ch a multiple of 20, plus 1 for tch.

Row 1: Sc in 2nd ch from hook and in each ch across, turn.

Row 2: Ch 1, sc in each sc across, turn.

Rows 3 and 4: Ch 3 (counts as dc here and throughout), 2 Crossed DC, *sc in next 10 sc**, 5 crossed DC, rep from * across, ending last rep at **, 2 Crossed DC, dc in last st, turn.

Rows 5 and 6: Rep Row 2.

Rows 7 and 8: Ch 1, sc in first 5 sc, *5 crossed DC**, sc in next 10 sc, rep from * across, ending last rep at **, sc in last 5 sts, turn.

Rows 9 and 10: Rep Row 2.
Rep Rows 3–10 for patt.

Size Medium:
Ch a multiple of 24, plus 1 for tch.

Row 1: Ch 1, sc in 2nd ch from hook and in each ch across, turn.

Row 2: Ch 1 sc in each sc across, turn.

Rows 3 and 4: Ch 3 (counts as dc here and throughout), dc in next sc, *2 Crossed DC, sc in next 12 sc**, 6 Crossed DC, rep from * across, ending last rep at **, 2 Crossed DC, dc in last 2 sts, turn.

Rows 5 and 6: Rep Row.

Rows 7 and 8: Ch 1, sc in first 6 sc, *6 Crossed DC**, sc in next 12 sc, rep form * across, ending last rep at **, sc in last 6 sts, turn.

Rows 9 and 10: Rep Row 2.
Rep Rows 3–10 for patt.

Size Large:
Ch a multiple of 28, plus 1 for tch.

Row 1: Sc in 2nd ch from hook and in each ch across, turn.

Row 2: Ch 1, sc in each sc across, turn.

Rows 3 and 4: Ch 3 (counts as dc here and throughout), 3 Crossed DC, *sc in next 14 sc**, 7 Crossed DC, rep from * across, ending last rep at **, 3 Crossed DC, dc in last st, turn.

Rows 5 and 6: Rep Row 2.

Rows 7 and 8: Ch 1, sc in next 7 sc, *7 Crossed DC**, sc in next 14 sc, rep from * across, ending last rep at **, sc in last 7 sts, turn.

Rows 9 and 10: Rep Row 2.
Rep Rows 3–10 for patt.

All Sizes:

❖ DECREASING IN PATTERN
When row begins and ends with sc, dec at beginning of a row by working ch 1, sk next sc; dec at end of the row by working sc2tog in last 2 sts.

When row begins and ends with dc, dec at beginning of row by working ch (2, dc in next st) (counts as dc2tog); dec at end of row by working dc2tog in last 2 sts. Continue in pattern, aligning Crossed DC's over previous rows to maintain pattern, and working a dc at beg and end of row to fill in as necessary.

❖ INCREASING IN PATTERN
When row begins and ends with sc, inc by working 2 sc in first or last st as directed.

When row begins and ends with dc, inc at beginning of row by working ch 3, dc in first st; inc at end of row by working 2 dc in last st, adding Crossed DC's in pattern as extra sts are added.

See diagrams on page 83 for decreases and increases.

FINISHED MEASUREMENTS
Bust 32 (38½, 45)"/81.5 (98, 114.5)cm

MATERIALS AND TOOLS
Crystal Palace Yarns Mini Mochi (80% merino 20% nylon; 1.75 oz/50g = 195 yd/176m): 8 (11, 13) balls, color 117 Beach Scene—approx 1560(2145, 2535) yds/1408(1936, 2288)m of fingering weight yarn; **❶**

Crochet hook: 3.25 mm (size D-3 U.S.)

1 button, approximately ½"/22mm diameter

Smaller button to sew to back of button flap

Sewing needle and matching sewing thread

GAUGE (AFTER BLOCKING)
20 sts in patt = 4"/10.2cm; 8 rows in patt = 2"/5cm

Note: Measure row gauge from beg of Row 4 to beg of Row 11

Always take time to check your gauge.

Special Abbreviations

Crossed DC: Sk next st, dc in next st, working over dc just made dc in last skipped st.

sc2tog: [insert hook in next st, yo and draw up a loop] twice, yo, draw yarn through 3 loops.

sc3tog: [insert hook in next st, yo and draw up a loop] 3 times, yo, draw yarn through 4 loops.

dc2tog: [yo, insert hook in next st, yo and draw up a loop, yo, draw yarn through 2 loops on hook] twice, yo, draw yarn through 3 loops.

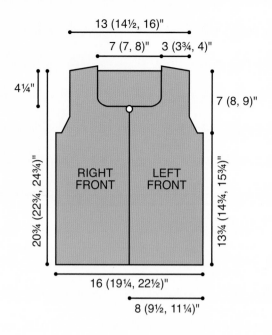

13 (14½, 16)"

7 (7, 8)" 3 (3¾, 4)"

4¼"

7 (8, 9)"

20¾ (22¾, 24¾)"

RIGHT
FRONT

LEFT
FRONT

13¾ (14¾, 15¾)"

16 (19¼, 22½)"

8 (9½, 11¼)"

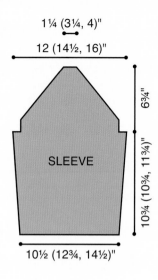

1¼ (3¼, 4)"

12 (14½, 16)"

6¾"

SLEEVE

10¾ (10¾, 11¾)"

10½ (12¾, 14½)"

Instructions

Back
Ch 81 (97, 113)

ROWS 1–55 (59, 63): Work even in patt—4 patt reps; 80 (96, 112) sts.

Armhole Shaping
ROW 1: Sl st over first 4 (5, 7) sts, starting in same st, work in established patt across to last 3 (4, 6) sts, turn, leaving rem sts unworked—74 (88, 100) sts.

ROW 2-6 (9, 11): Dec 1 st at each end of every row—64 (72, 80) sts at end of last row.

ROW 7-28 (10-32, 12-36): Work even in established patt.

Right Shoulder Shaping
ROW 1: Sl st over first 3 (4, 5) sts, sc in next 3 (4, 5) sts, hdc in next 4 (5, 5) sts, dc in next 4 (5, 5) sts, turn—11 (14, 15) sts.

ROW 2: Ch 2, hdc in next 4 (5, 6) sts, sc in next 5 (7, 8) sts, sl st to next sc—10 (13, 14) sts. Fasten off.

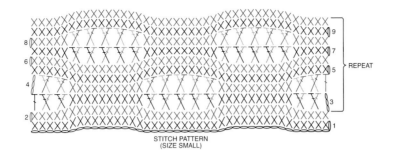

STITCH PATTERN
(SIZE SMALL)

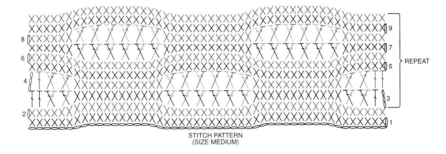

STITCH PATTERN
(SIZE MEDIUM)

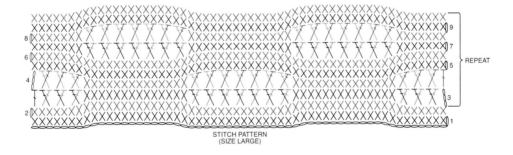

STITCH PATTERN
(SIZE LARGE)

INCREASING AT BEG AND
END OF ROWS ENDING IN DC

INCREASING AT BEG AND
END OF ROWS ENDING IN SC

DECREASING AT BEG AND
END OF ROWS ENDING IN DC

DECREASING AT BEG AND
END OF ROWS ENDING IN SC

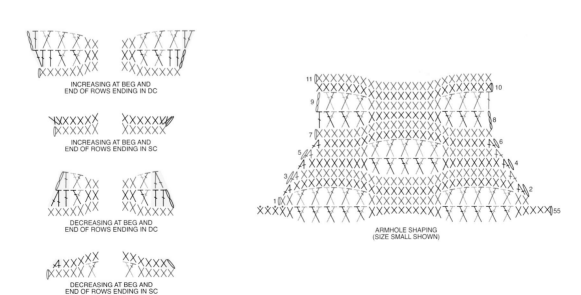

ARMHOLE SHAPING
(SIZE SMALL SHOWN)

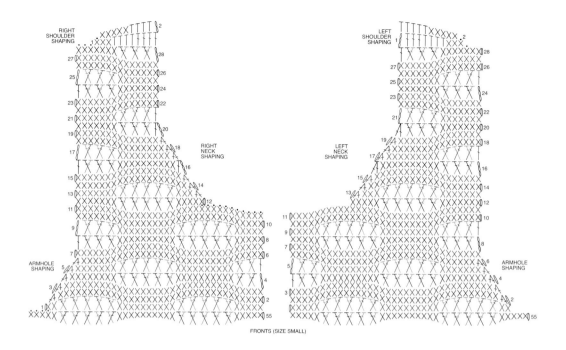

FRONTS (SIZE SMALL)

Left Shoulder Shaping

With WS facing, join yarn in 14th (18th, 20th) st from end of last row of body.

ROW 1: Ch 3, dc in next 3 (4, 4) sts, hdc in next st, turn—11 (14, 15) sts.

ROW 2: Ch 1, sl st in next sc, sc in next 5 (7, 8) sts, hdc in next 4, (5, 6) sts—10 (13, 14) sts. Fasten off.

Right Front

Ch 41 (49, 57).

ROW 1-55 (59, 63): Work even in patt—2 patt reps; 40 (48, 56) sts.

Armhole Shaping

ROW 1: Sl st over first 4 (5, 7) sts, starting in same st, work in established patt across, turn—37 (44, 50) sts.

ROWS 2–6 (9, 11): Maintaining established patt, dec 1 st at armhole edge—32 (36, 40) sts at end of last row.

ROWS 7–11 (10–15, 12–19): Work even in established patt.

Neckline Shaping

ROW 12 (16, 20): Sl st over first 11 (15, 17) sts, starting in same st, work in established patt across, turn—22 (22, 24) sts.

ROWS 13–20 (17–20, 21–24): Work in established patt, dec 1 st at neck edge—14 (18, 20) sts at end of last row.

ROWS 21–28 (21–32, 25–36): Work even in established patt.

Right Shoulder Shaping

Rep back right shoulder shaping.

Armhole Shaping

ROW 1: Work in established patt across to last 3 (4, 6) sts, turn, leaving rem sts unworked—37 (44, 50) sts.

ROWS 2–6 (9, 11): Maintaining established patt, dec 1 st at armhole edge across —32 (36, 40) sts at end of last row.

ROWS 7–11 (10–15, 12–19): Work even in established patt.

Neckline Shaping

ROW 12 (16, 20): Work in established patt across to last 10 (14, 16) sts, turn, leaving rem sts unworked—22 (22, 24) sts.

ROWS 13–20 (17–20, 21–24): Work in established patt, dec 1 st at neck edge—14 (18, 20) sts at end of last row.

ROWS 21–28 (21–32, 25–36): Work even in established patt.

Left Shoulder Shaping

Rep back left shoulder shaping.

Sleeve

Ch 53 (65, 73).

ROW 1: Sc in 2nd ch and in each ch across—52 (64, 72) sts.

ROW 2: Ch 1, sc in each sc across, turn.

Size M only:

ROWS 3 AND 4: Ch 1, sc in first 2 sc, *6 Crossed DC**, sc in next 12 sts, rep from * across ending last rep at **, sc in last 2 sc, turn.

ROWS 5 AND 6: Rep Row 2.

ROWS 7 AND 8: Ch 3, dc in next sc, *sc in next 12 sc**, 6 Crossed DC, rep from * across, ending last rep at **, dc in last 2 sts, turn.

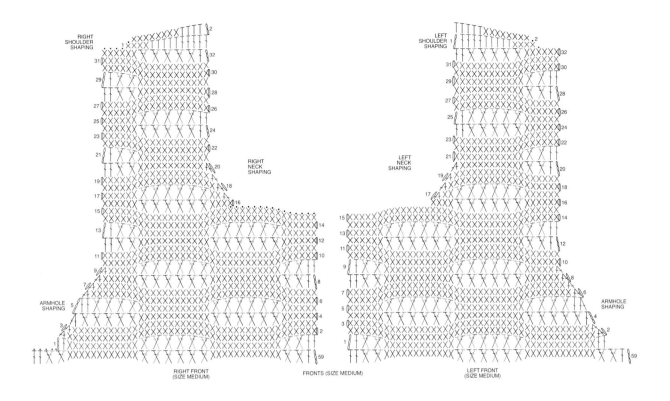

RIGHT SHOULDER SHAPING

RIGHT NECK SHAPING

LEFT SHOULDER SHAPING

LEFT NECK SHAPING

ARMHOLE SHAPING

ARMHOLE SHAPING

RIGHT FRONT (SIZE MEDIUM)

FRONTS (SIZE MEDIUM)

LEFT FRONT (SIZE MEDIUM)

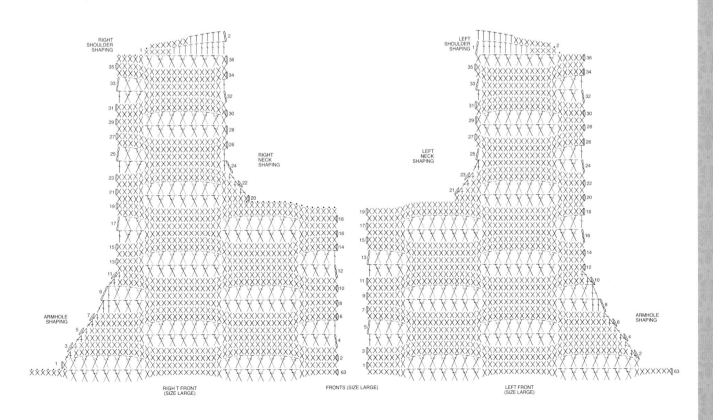

RIGHT SHOULDER SHAPING

RIGHT NECK SHAPING

LEFT SHOULDER SHAPING

LEFT NECK SHAPING

ARMHOLE SHAPING

ARMHOLE SHAPING

RIGH T FRONT (SIZE LARGE)

FRONTS (SIZE LARGE)

LEFT FRONT (SIZE LARGE)

Size L only:

ROWS 3 AND 4: Ch 1, *7 Crossed DC**, sc in next 14 sts, rep from * across ending last rep at **, sc in last sc, turn.

ROWS 5 AND 6: Rep Row 2.

ROWS 7 AND 8: Ch 3, *sc in next 14 sc**, 7 Crossed DC, rep from * across, ending last rep at **, dc in last st, turn.

All Sizes:

ROW 9: Work even in established patt.

ROW 10: Inc 1 st on each end.

ROWS 11–22: Maintaining established patt, inc 1 st on each end of every 4th row, with last increase on Row 22, ending with 60 (72, 80) sts.

ROWS 23–43 (43, 47): Work even in established patt.

Sleeve Cap

ROW 1: Ch 1, sl st over first 4 (5, 7) sc, starting in same st, work in established patt across to within last 3 (4, 6) sts, turn, leaving rem sts unworked—54 (64, 68) sts.

ROWS 2–5: Work even in established patt.

ROWS 6–25: Work in established patt, dec 1 st at each end of every row—14 (24, 28) sts at end of last row.

ROW 26: Ch 1, sc3tog over first 3 sts, sc in each st across to last 3 sts, sc3tog over last 3 sts, turn—10 (20, 24) sts.

ROW 27: Ch 1, sc3tog over first 3 sts, sc in each st across to last 3 sts, sc3tog over last 3 sts—6 (16, 20) sts.

Collar

ROW 1: With RS facing, join yarn at top right-hand corner of Right Front, ch 1, sc in first sc, sc evenly across to top left-hand corner of Left Front, turn.

ROW 2: Ch 1, *sc in first sc, 2 sc in next sc, rep from * across, turn.

ROW 3: Ch 3, sk first st, dc in each sc across, turn.

ROW 4: Ch 4, sk first st, tr in each dc across, turn.

Right Front Edging

ROW 1: With RS facing, join yarn in bottom corner of Right Front edge, ch 1, sc evenly across Right Front edge to base of collar. Fasten off.

Left Front Edging

ROW 1: With RS facing, join yarn at top corner of Left Front edge at base of collar, ch 1, sc evenly across Left Front edge to bottom corner. Fasten off.

Button Flap

ROW 1: With RS facing, join yarn 1 st below base of collar on Left Front edge, ch 1, sc in next 4 sts, turn

ROWS 2–3: Ch 1, sc in each sc across, turn. Fasten off.

Note: The size of the flap can be adjusted if your button is larger. Sew the button close to the lapel edge.

Button Loop

ROW 1: With WS facing, join yarn on Right Front edge opposite button flap, 2 sts below collar, ch 7, sk next 2 sts, sl st to next st, ch 1, sl st to next st on lapel edge, turn.

ROW 2: Work 6 or 7 sc in next ch-7 loop, sl st in lapel edge. Fasten off.

Note: The size of this loop may also be adjusted for your button size.

With sewing needle and thread, sew the larger button to button flap, using the smaller button on the back of the flap to stabilize.

FIJI CARDI GOT ITS NAME from the lovely wave-like stitch pattern and the watery colors in this self-striping, sport-weight yarn. The design is a standard bottom-up, set-in sleeve, with a fairly wide and deep round neckline. It is short in length, has no waist shaping, with a three-quarter-length sleeve. It is designed to be close fitting. Make it with any sport-weight yarn.

Construction Details

The interesting element in this sweater is the very long stitch pattern consisting of 20 stitches and measuring 4"/10.2cm (for size Small). The wave pattern runs all the way from the beginning of one front piece, across the side seam, around the back, then on to the other front section. Because of this, it's not possible to simply make the back and front pieces a couple of inches/cm larger without destroying the neat symmetry of the stitch pattern.

The clever way around this built-in limitation is to make the stitch pattern larger for different sizes. Instead of basing the pattern repeat on 20 stitches, it can become 24, or 28. The waves will be larger as the size increases.

Fit and Choosing Your Size

The three sizes given here should make it possible for people with a bust width between 30"/76.2cm and 45"/114.5cm to find a suitable size. Choose your size according to bust width, rather than shoulder width, on this pattern. Since the front of the sweater only closes at the top, the question of ease at the bust is not so important—wearing the sweater open gives the garment ease.

LESSON 8: Adjusting Size by Changing Gauge

If you don't feel right with any of these sizes you can change the gauge to get different measurements. While each size is currently at the same gauge, the pattern repeat (PR) measures different lengths, as follows:

    Small: PR is 20 stitches = 4"/10.2cm
    Medium: PR is 24 stitches = 4⅘"/12.2cm
    Large: PR is 28 stitches = 5⅗"/14.2cm

Suppose you want a finished bust size of 42"/106.7cm; that would be 21"/53.3cm across the back. Since all sizes have 4 PR across the back width, you can easily calculate the width you would need each PR to be:

    21"/53.3cm divided by 4 = 5¼"/13.34cm

Looking at the pattern repeat measurements above, the easy fix is to work the Medium pattern repeat of 24 stitches at a looser gauge. You could also work the Large pattern repeat of 28 stitches somewhat tighter than gauge. The choice would depend on whether you want to use a slightly lighter or heavier yarn. The yarn used here is a sport weight. A DK-weight yarn will look great at a slightly looser gauge, but swatch first to see if you still have good drape with heavier yarn.

If you do gauge up and use the Medium as your pattern, your new gauge is 24 stitches = 5¼"/13.34cm. Consider how this will affect other crucial measurements, particularly the shoulder. Size Medium has 72 stitches at the shoulder, measuring 14½"/36.8cm. With your new gauge, the shoulder will measure 15¾"/40cm. If you need it a bit smaller, you can alter the armhole, decreasing a few more stitches to make the shoulder width smaller; refer to Lesson 7: Master Class in Fitted Armholes (page 77). These changes at the armhole must be done the same on the Back and both Front pieces. If you use this new gauge on the size Small you'll have a garment that measures 17½"/44.5cm across the back with a finished bust of 35"/88.9cm, and shoulder width will be 14"/35.6cm. For both these sizes, a larger gauge will make all the measurements increase by about 10 percent, including the neck width, which on this open-necked sweater will look fine.

To plot out the entire sweater including sleeves at your new gauge, consult Shaping and Alteration 101 (page 34).

LESSON 9: Master Class On Armholes and Sleeve Caps

Alteration on a garment will often require corresponding changes at the armhole. The adjustments may be quite small, perhaps only 1 to 3"/ 5 to 7.6cm. The designer has done most of the difficult math already, and any changes you make are merely tweaks. Nevertheless, an understanding of how these parts relate can help you get the neat look of a well-fitted armhole and sleeve cap.

The alterations that have implications for armhole and sleeve cap are:

1. Widening of the bust in relation to the shoulder
2. Narrowing the shoulder in relation to the bust
3. Widening of the sleeve

The main consideration when adjusting sleeve caps and armholes is that the perimeters must be close to the same, with the cap measuring up to 2"/5cm more. That's because the sleeve cap will be sewn into the armhole. The two shapes are different, as you can see in the schematics on page 82, but so long as their perimeters are of similar length, they will flow over the top of the arm and torso very nicely when sewn together. Any bit of extra fabric in the sleeve cap can be eased in while sewing.

> ## note
> The perimeter of the front and back armholes must match or be close to the perimeter of the sleeve cap; the latter can be slightly larger. The extra inches/cm are eased in when sewing the two parts together.

ALTERING A SLEEVE CAP TO MATCH A WIDER ARMHOLE

In Lesson 7: Master Class in Fitted Armholes (page 77), we discussed how to make armholes wider or deeper. In a garment with sleeves, any changes in the armhole will require corresponding changes in the sleeve cap.

The perimeter of the armhole consists of the measurements of all three sections we discussed in Lesson 7: the initial bind off, the tapered section, and the straight section.

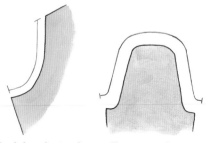

Armhole perimeter x2   Sleeve cap perimeter

Figure 1

This measurement is not shown on a schematic. The schematic will tell you the armhole depth, but the perimeter will be 1 to 4"/2.5 to 10.2cm larger. That's because the tapered section, running on a diagonal, is longer than a straight line. (Remember, armhole depth is measured as a straight line from the top of the shoulder to the bottom of the armhole).

The simplest way to get a measurement for the armhole perimeter is to make your back piece and measure it with a tape measure. Since the front of the garment will have the same armhole, you simply multiply by two and you'll have the perimeter (figure 1).

The perimeter of the sleeve cap consists of the initial bind off, the two tapered sides of the cap, and the top of the cap. Designers usually do considerable math to work out matching perimeters of armholes and sleeve caps for all sizes. Alterations, however, are small tweaks and complex math can usually be avoided.

If you've made a larger size up to the armhole, but need a smaller shoulder width than is indicated for your size, you will be decreasing more in the second part of the armhole, where tapering removes stitches gradually for a few rows. You'll have more of those tapering rows, and therefore your armhole will be wider than the original armhole. It will also have a slightly larger perimeter than the original. The change in measurement should not be great, only the difference between a slanted edge and a straight edge, perhaps 2 or 3"/5 or 7.6cm at most.

You will need to alter the sleeve cap so its circumference matches the larger one you now have at the armhole. To make the cap taller, add rows at the start of the cap, right after the bound off stitches that begin the armhole, adding enough rows to increase the perimeter of the sleeve cap by the same number of inches/cm.

What if you have made an alteration in width to the sleeve? Suppose you have added 10 stitches to the bicep width. If you continue working the sleeve as instructed, those 10 stitches will remain at the top of the cap. This will add to the perimeter of the cap and may make it too large. Instead, decrease more rapidly on the cap than indicated in the pattern,

so that you match the final stitch count at the top of the cap. Because you have a more slanted edge along the cap, it will be longer in perimeter and will be closer to the perimeter of the altered armhole (figure 2).

note

For the mathematically-minded reader who craves more in-depth knowledge of this topic, I refer you to a magnificent article by Jenna Wilson on knitty.com: http://www.knitty.com/ISSUEfall04/FEATfall04TBP.html

Here's a suggestion that will allow you to make adjustments before finishing your pieces to insure against any mismatches of armhole and sleeve cap perimeters. Work the back and front pieces of the cardigan, including your alterations to the armhole shaping, but don't work the shoulder shaping rows. Work your sleeve cap with any alterations up to Row 25, and measure its perimeter. Then measure the two armholes on your pieces and see if they are close to the same as the cap. Keep in mind that the sleeve cap can be up to 2"/5cm more in perimeter. Now, if your perimeters work out, you're good to go and can continue

with the shoulder shaping rows and the top of the sleeve cap.

If the armhole needs to be bigger to accommodate your new cap, add a few more rows (worked even) to the back and front pieces until you get the right fit. The armholes on this garment are on the small side, so adding a bit here will not do any harm. If the armhole is larger than the cap, make the cap a little taller by adding a few rows worked even between Rows 25 and 26. Once you've achieved the correct numbers for the perimeters, work the shoulder shaping and the top of the cap, and sew your pieces together.

Nothing is more elegant than a well-fitting armhole and sleeve cap on a crochet garment. I've seen too many photos of pieces where fabric is bagging in this area. Yet once you get to know your body measurements and the techniques described here, it's very possible to have perfect fit in this area every time. You'll get to know what are typical sleeve cap heights and widths for your body, and can judge from the pattern's schematic whether it will work for you. You will understand how to make the caps wider or narrower at the top, or taller. Your understanding of shaping armholes will progress as well. The individual elements are really not too complicated, and once you've put the pieces together a few times, you'll have excellent control of your finished garments.

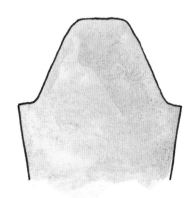

Original sleeve cap

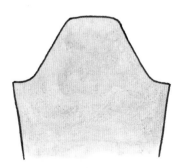

Shorter cap with more rapid decreases

Figure 2

BEAU BLAZER
fitted sleeve jacket

The angled stitch pattern in this sweater creates visual interest and makes for some intriguing shaping techniques.

Stitch Pattern

Ch multiple of 7 plus 1.

Row 1: 2 dc in 4th ch from hook, *sk 3 ch, sc in next ch, ch 2, dc in next 3 ch, rep from * across, ending sc in last ch, turn.

Row 2: Ch 3, 2 dc in first sc, sk next 3 dc, sc in top of next ch-2, ch 2, 3 dc in same ch-2, *sk next (sc, 3 dc), sc in top of next ch-2, ch 2, 3 dc in same ch-2, rep from * across, ending sc in tch, turn.

Rep row 2 for patt.

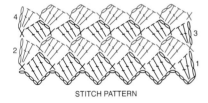

STITCH PATTERN

Special Notes

1. The stitch pattern used in this design begins with a starting chain that functions in an unusual way. Some of the chains become the edge of your first tilted squares. For this reason, make the chain stitches in the foundation tighter than usual and remember that the starting chain does not represent the actual width of the work after completing Row 1. The first row will be slightly wider than those that follow, causing a natural flare at the bottom of the garment. This note is applicable to the Back and Front pieces, but not the sleeve. Work the starting chain for sleeves at normal tension.

2. Because of the angled nature of this pattern, shaping happens at the beginning of a row, not at the end. Consequently it happens 1 row apart on left and right sides. For example, on Left Front shaping occurs 1 row before it does on Right Front. The method works in this angled pattern because the first pattern in the row shifts down to actually become part of the previous row. The outcome will look almost the same on both sides—perhaps ¼"/6mm different, which can be adjusted in blocking.

3. Partial pattern repeats at the beginning of rows do not count as a pattern repeat.

4. Counting rows can be tricky! When you are shaping with slip stitches at the beginning of a row, the decrease actually appears on the prior row. Also, the first half-pattern repeat appears a bit lower than the others in the row. To avoid errors, count rows in the center of your fabric.

FINISHED MEASUREMENTS

Bust 32 (36, 40, 44, 48, 52)"/81.5 (91.5, 101.5, 112, 122, 132)cm

MATERIALS AND TOOLS

Knit Picks Andean Silk (55% alpaca, 23% silk, 22% merino; 1.75oz/50g = 96 yd/86m): 14 (17, 19, 21, 24, 26) balls, color Crimini—approx 1344 (1632, 1824, 2016, 2304, 2496)yds /1210 (1462, 1634, 1806, 2064, 2236)m of worsted weight yarn; (4)

Crochet hooks: 4.0 mm (size G-6 U.S.), 3.75 mm (size F-5 U.S.) hook

1 button, approximately ½"/22mm diameter

1 shank button of your choice, approx 1¼"/32mm in diameter

GAUGE

With larger hook, 4 patt reps (measured from sc to sc) and 8 rows in patt = 4"/10.2cm

With smaller hook, 4 patt reps and 8 rows in patt = 3 3/4"/9.5cm

Always take time to check your gauge.

Special Abbreviations

Patt Rep = sc in top of next ch-2, ch 2, 3 dc in same ch-2 sp.

Dec 1 patt rep = do not ch 1 at start of dec row, sk first sc, sl st over next 3 dc, work patt rep in next ch-2 sp.

Note: This dec 1 removes the partial Patt Rep that begins the row. For this reason, the Patt Rep count does not go down in the row where the decrease is made, but on the following row.

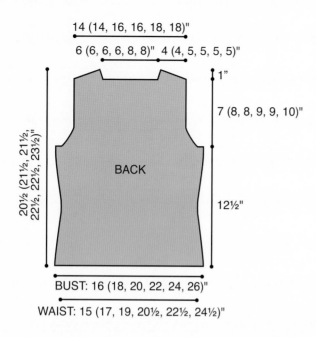

14 (14, 16, 16, 18, 18)"

6 (6, 6, 6, 8, 8)"   4 (4, 5, 5, 5, 5)"

1"

7 (8, 8, 9, 9, 10)"

20½ (21½, 21½, 22½, 22½, 23½)"

BACK

12½"

BUST: 16 (18, 20, 22, 24, 26)"

WAIST: 15 (17, 19, 20½, 22½, 24½)"

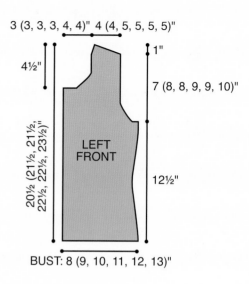

3 (3, 3, 3, 4, 4)" 4 (4, 5, 5, 5, 5)"

4½"

1"

7 (8, 8, 9, 9, 10)"

20½ (21½, 21½, 22½, 22½, 23½)"

LEFT FRONT

12½"

BUST: 8 (9, 10, 11, 12, 13)"

Instructions

Back

With larger hook, ch 120 (134, 148, 162, 176, 190)

ROWS 1–9: Work even in patt—16 (18, 20, 22, 24, 26) patt reps.

Waist Shaping

ROWS 10–15: Change to smaller hook, work even in patt.

Waist to Bust Shaping

ROWS 16–26: Change to larger hook, work even in patt.

Armhole Shaping

Sizes S, M and L only:

ROW 1 (RS): Dec 1 patt rep, cont in patt across, sc in tch, turn—16 (18, 20) patt reps.

ROW 2: Dec 1 patt rep, cont in patt across, sc in next ch-2 sp, turn—15 (17, 19) patt reps.

Size S only:

ROW 3: Work even in patt across—14 patt reps.

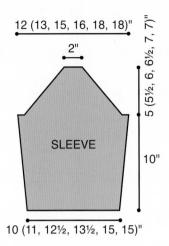

12 (13, 15, 16, 18, 18)"

2"

5 (5½, 6, 6½, 7, 7)"

SLEEVE

10"

10 (11, 12½, 13½, 15, 15)"

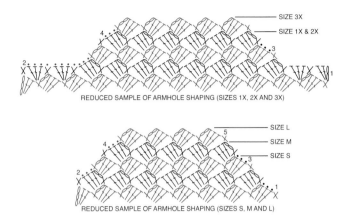

SIZE 3X
SIZE 1X & 2X

REDUCED SAMPLE OF ARMHOLE SHAPING (SIZES 1X, 2X AND 3X)

SIZE L
SIZE M
SIZE S

REDUCED SAMPLE OF ARMHOLE SHAPING (SIZES S, M AND L)

Sizes M and L:

ROWS 3-4: Rep row 2 (twice)—15 (17) patt reps.

ROW 5: Work even in patt across—14 (16) patt reps.

Sizes 1X, 2X and 3X only:

ROW 1 (RS): Ch 2, 2 dc in first sc, sc in top of next ch-2, 3 dc in next sc, work 19 (21, 23) patt reps, [sc in top of next ch 2, 3 dc in next sc] twice, sc in tch, turn—19 (21, 23) patt reps.

ROW 2: Sk first sc, sl st over next 11 sts, work 18 (20, 22) patt reps, turn.

ROW 3: Dec 1 patt rep, cont in patt across to last patt rep, sc in top of last ch-2, turn—17 (19, 21) patt reps, turn.

Sizes 1X and 2X only:

ROW 4: Work even in patt across—16 (18) patt reps.

Size 3X only:

ROWS 4-5: Rep row 3 (twice)—19 patt reps.

ROW 6: Work even in patt across—18 patt reps.

All Sizes:

There are now 3 (5, 5, 4, 4, 6) rows of shaping completed at armhole.

Work 11 (11, 11, 14, 14, 14) rows even on 14 (14, 16, 16, 18, 18) patt reps.

There are now 14 (16, 16, 18, 18, 20) rows at armhole.

Shoulder Shaping

Sizes S and M only:

ROW 1 (RS): Dec 1 patt rep, work in patt across—14 (14) patt reps.

ROW 2: Dec 1 patt rep, work in patt across—13 (13) patt reps.

Sizes L, 1X, 2X, and 3X only:

ROW 1 (RS): Ch 3, 2 dc in sc, sc in next ch-2 sp, work in patt for 15 (15, 17, 17) patt reps, sc in next ch-2 sp, 3 dc in next sc, sc in tch, turn.

ROW 2: Sk first sc, sl st over next 7 sts, work in patt for 14 (14, 16, 16) patt reps, turn—14 (14, 16, 16) patt reps.

All Sizes:

ROW 3: Dec 1 patt rep, work in patt for 3 patt reps, *sc in top of next ch-2, 3 dc in next sc**, sc in top of next ch 2, 2 dc in next sc, rep from * 2 (2, 2, 2, 3, 3) times, rep from * to ** 0 (0, 1, 1, 1, 1) time, work 3 patt reps, sc in top of next ch-2, turn.

Left Shoulder

ROW 4: Dec 1 patt, *sc in top of next ch-2, 3 dc in next sc, sc in top of next ch-2, ch 2, 3 dc in same ch-2 sp, sc in top of next ch-2, turn.

ROW 5: Ch 3, 2 dc in first sc, sl st to next ch-2 sp. Fasten off.

Right Shoulder

ROW 4: With WS facing, sk first patt rep on opposite shoulder, join yarn at top of first ch-2 sp, sc in top of ch-2 sp, ch 2, 3 dc in same ch-2 sp, sc in top of next ch-2 sp, 3 dc next sc, sc in top of next ch-2, turn.

ROW 5: Sk first sc, sl st in next 4 sts, ch 3, 2 dc in same sc, sl st to next ch-2 sp. Fasten off.

Left Front

With larger hook, ch 64 (71, 78, 85, 92, 99).

ROW 1–26: Work same as Back through row 26—8 (9, 10, 11, 12, 13) patt reps.

Armhole Shaping

Sizes S, M and L only:

ROW 1 (RS): Dec 1 patt rep, cont in patt across, sc in tch, turn—8 (9, 10) patt reps.

ROW 2: Work even in patt, turn—7 (8, 9) patt reps.

Sizes M and L only:

ROWS 3 AND 4: Rep rows 1 and 2—7 (8) patt reps.

Sizes 1X, 2X and 3X only:

ROW 1: Ch 2, 2 dc in sc, sc in top of next ch-2, 3 dc in next sc, work 10 (11, 12) patt reps, sc in top of tch, turn.

ROW 2: Work in patt across, turn—9 (10, 11) patt reps.

ROW 3: Dec 1 patt rep, cont in patt across—9 (10, 11) patt reps.

ROW 4: Rep rows 2—8 (9, 10) patt reps.

Size 3X only:

ROWS 5 AND 6: Rep rows 3 and 4—9 patt reps.

All Sizes:

There are now 2 (4, 4, 4, 4, 6) rows of shaping completed at armhole. Work 8 (8, 8, 10, 10, 10) rows even on 7 (7, 8, 8, 9, 9) patt reps. There are now 10 (12, 12, 14, 14, 16) rows at armhole.

Neckline Shaping

ROW 1: Work in patt completing 5 patt reps, turn, leaving rem sts unworked—5 patt reps.

ROW 2: Dec 1 patt rep, cont in patt across—4 patt reps.

ROWS 3 AND 4: Work even in patt.

Shoulder Shaping

ROW 1: Ch 3, 2 dc in first sc, work in patt for 4 patt reps, sc in top of ch-2, turn.

ROW 2: Ch 3, 2 dc in first sc, work in patt for 3 patt reps, sc in top of next ch-2, turn—3 patt reps.

ROW 3: Dec 1 patt rep, work in patt for 3 patt reps, sc in tch, turn—3 patt reps.

ROW 4: Dec 1 patt rep, work in patt for 1 patt rep, sc in next ch-2 ps, 3 dc in next sc, sc in top of next ch-2, turn.

ROW 5: Sk first sc, sl st in next 4 sts, ch 3, 2 dc in same sc, sl st to next ch-2 sp. Fasten off.

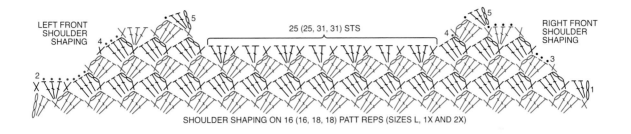

LEFT FRONT SHOULDER SHAPING

RIGHT FRONT SHOULDER SHAPING

25 (25, 31, 31) STS

SHOULDER SHAPING ON 16 (16, 18, 18) PATT REPS (SIZES L, 1X AND 2X)

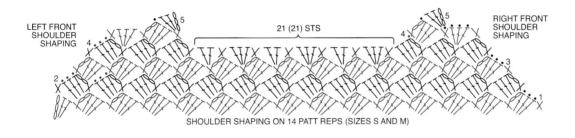

LEFT FRONT SHOULDER SHAPING

RIGHT FRONT SHOULDER SHAPING

21 (21) STS

SHOULDER SHAPING ON 14 PATT REPS (SIZES S AND M)

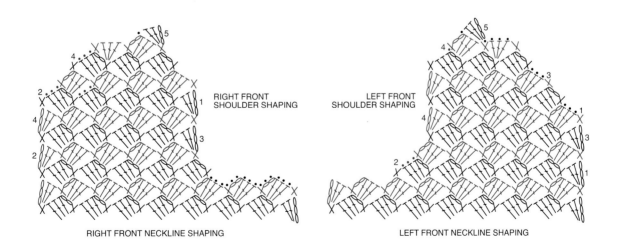

RIGHT FRONT SHOULDER SHAPING

LEFT FRONT SHOULDER SHAPING

RIGHT FRONT NECKLINE SHAPING

LEFT FRONT NECKLINE SHAPING

Right Front

Work same as Back through row 26—8 (9, 10, 11, 12, 13) patt reps.

Armhole Shaping

Sizes S, M and L only:

ROW 1: Work in patt across, turn—8 (9, 10) patt reps.

ROW 2: Dec 1 patt rep, work in patt across—8 (9, 10) patt reps.

ROW 3: Work in patt across, turn—7 (8, 9) patt reps.

Sizes M and L only:

ROWS 4 AND 5: Rep rows 2 and 3—7 (8) patt reps.

Sizes 1X, 2X and 3X only:

ROW 1: Ch 3, 2 dc in first sc, work in even patt across 9 (10, 11) patt reps, [sc in top of next ch-2 sp, 3 dc in next sc] twice, sc in tch, turn—9 (10, 11) patt reps.

ROW 2: Sk first sc, sl st in each of next 11 sts, work in patt across 9 (10, 11) patt reps, turn.

ROW 3: Work even in patt across, turn—8 (9, 10) patt reps.

Size 3X only:

ROW 4: Dec 1 patt rep, work in patt across—10 patt reps.

ROW 5: Rep rows 3—9 patt reps.

All Sizes:

There are now 3 (5, 5, 3, 3, 5) rows of shaping completed at armhole. Work 7 (7, 7, 11, 11, 11) rows even on 7 (7, 8, 8, 9, 9) patt reps. There are now 10 (12, 12, 14, 14, 16) rows at armhole.

Neckline Shaping

ROW 1: Sl st over 15 (15, 15, 15, 21, 21) sts, sc in next ch-2, work in patt across—6 patt reps.

ROW 2: Work in patt completing 5 patt reps, turn.

ROWS 3 AND 4: Work even in patt.

Shoulder Shaping

ROW 1: Ch 3, 2 dc in first sc, work in patt working 4 patt reps, sc in top of next ch-2 sp, 3 dc in next sc, sc in tch, turn—4 patt reps.

ROW 2: Sk first sc, sl st in next 7 sts, work in patt across 4 patt reps, sc in tch, turn—4 patt reps.

ROW 3: Dec 1 patt rep, work in patt across 3 patt reps, sc in top of next ch-2, turn—3 patt reps.

ROW 4: Dec 1 patt rep, sc in top of ch-2, 3 dc in next sc, work 1 patt rep, sc in top of ch-2, turn—1 patt rep.

ROW 5: Ch 3, 2 dc in first sc, sc in top of ch-2. Fasten off.

Sleeve (make 2)

Note: The sleeve begins with a variation of the st patt to create tighter edge.

With smaller hook, ch 40 (43, 49, 52, 58, 58).
ROW 1: 2 dc in 4th ch from hook, *sk next 2 ch, (sc, ch-2, 2 dc) in next ch, rep from * across to last 3 ch, sk mext 2 ch, sc in last ch, turn—12 (13, 15, 16, 18, 18) patt reps
ROWS 2–8: Ch 3, 2 dc in sc, *sc in top of next ch-2, ch 2, 2 dc in same ch-2 sp, rep from * across, sc in tch.
ROW 9–22: Change to larger hook, work even in patt.

Cap

Sizes S, M and L:
ROW 1: Dec 1 patt rep, work in patt across—12 (13, 15) patt reps.
ROWS 2–10 (11, 12): Rep row 1, dec 1 patt rep on each row, ending with 3 patt reps.
ROW 11 (12, 13): Dec 1 patt rep, [3 dc in next sc, sc in next ch 2] 1 (2, 3) times. Fasten off.

Sizes 1X, 2X and 3X only:
ROW 1: Ch 2, 2 dc in sc, sc in top of next ch-2, 2 dc in next sc, work in patt across 13 (15, 15) patt reps, [sc in top of next ch-2, 3 dc in next sc] twice, sc in tch, turn.
ROW 2: Skip first sc, sl st in next 11 sts, work in patt across 13 (15, 15) patt reps
ROW 3: Dec 1 patt rep, cont in patt across, sc in top of ch-2, turn—12 (14, 14) patt reps.
ROWS 4–13 (14, 14): Rep row 4, dec 1 patt rep on each row, ending with 2 (3, 3) patt reps.
ROW 14 (15, 15): Dec 1 patt rep, [3 dc in next sc, sc in ch 2] 1 (2, 2) times. Fasten off.

Finishing

Wet block pieces to given measurements on schematic. As you pin wet pieces, press down on the fabric to flatten the "bumps." Check while drying that holes between patt reps don't get too large. This garment will definitely stretch with wear, so snug is better. After blocking, sew front to back at shoulders. Sew side seams. Sew sleeve seams. Set in sleeve.

Try on the garment. Mark the spot where you would like blazer to close. Because of the weight of the fabric, you may find that the back neck stretches 1"/2.5cm or so, making the shoulders a bit wide. To correct this, pull in the back neckline by working slip sts on the RS, from one shoulder seam to the other.

Using matching sewing thread, sew a button on left side of jacket, sewing through the fabric and into a smaller button on the WS of the fabric. With RS facing, tie on at opposite point on the right side, slightly below the center of the button. With E hook, ch 10, sl st to point 1"/2.5cm higher on right side, turn, sl st into each ch, sl st to starting point, end off.

Try on the jacket again. Fold back lapels and pin in place. Sew down with a few tacking sts.

Closure Options
There are several options for closing this garment in addition to the one shown. Instead of an open lapel, you can place a snap or button at the top of the front pieces to close it. For the folded-down lapel, you can place the button at a variety of places along the length of the front edges, either at the waist as shown, or just under the bust. Once you've determined this spot, mark it with a safety pin, sew on your button, and make your button loop. Then steam press the lapel so it stays flat and make a few discreet tacks at the top corner of the lapel.

THIS BLAZER IS MEANT to be a classic addition to your wardrobe. Its long V-neck and shaped waist create slimming lines. The sleeves are three-quarter length, and there is a natural flare at the very bottom that adds an extra 1½"/3.8cm of width at the hips for all sizes. The angled stitch pattern creates interesting texture, resembling a woven look.

Construction Details

This fitted-sleeve garment is made in five pieces: a Back, two Fronts, and two Sleeves. The front pieces meet at the center but don't overlap, and a single snazzy button closes the jacket at the waist. The neckline is fairly close in width and 4 to 5"/10.2 to 12.7cm deep. The points at the top of the front pieces fold down to create a lapel, and are tacked down for stability. Angled patterns—where the pattern repeats don't line up over one another in adjacent rows, but rather sit at an angle—are very attractive, breaking up the usual gridlike lines across the body. The natural angle in the pattern can be exploited to shape the garment. Several different strategies are used to shape this design, including changing hook size and internal shaping by changing the number of stitches in each pattern repetition.

Choosing Yarn

The yarn used for this project is worsted weight, made with a mix of fibers—alpaca, merino, and silk; it has some stretchiness yet also holds its shape. The silk content provides a lovely luster, and the loosely plied yarn looks particularly nice with this stitch pattern. Look for similar characteristics for any substitute yarns.

Fit and Choosing Your Size

Depending on your preferences, this design can be worked for either a close or relaxed fit at the bust line. Since the fronts don't close, natural ease is built-in. At the shoulders, stay close to your actual shoulder width. Even though it's a blazer and meant to be worn over other clothing, the weight of this garment will make the back of the neck stretch at least 1"/2.5cm or more, consequently increasing the shoulder width as well. The length at the

bottom can be at high hip or a few inches/centimeters lower. The sleeves can be lengthened as well, but shaping them to wrist width is not possible.

For this design, check the width of the shoulders, bust, and sleeves, and pick the size with the most width measurements that are closest to your own. If the sleeve widths and shoulder width work for you, but not the bust, this is a good pattern to learn how to create crochet's version of bust darts.

LESSON 10: Lengthening Sleeves in an Angled Pattern

You can lengthen the sleeves on this garment, but they are not suitable for further tapering to wrist width. A wider sleeve at the bottom is fine, but keep in mind that you can also gather it with a cuff at the bottom.

For this alteration, begin by referring to your full sleeve measurement. Subtract the sleeve length on the schematic from your own sleeve length to determine how many more inches/centimeters are needed.

Lengthen the sleeve by repeating the pattern used in Row 1 for as many inches/centimeters as you need. After you've added the extra rows, work one row as in Row 2 of the pattern then continue with the instructions as written.

You'll probably have a different row gauge for this section, so measure your work as you go rather than depending on the row gauge in the pattern. Work a few rows to see how many are needed for 1"/2.5cm and then keep measuring until you get the correct number of extra inches/centimeters.

To create a cuff that will draw in the sleeve to wrist width, work an edging of single crochet stitches. Start by swatching and getting a gauge for your sc stitches and then figure out how many you will need for your wrist width plus about 2"/5cm of ease. Figure out the difference in the number of stitches you have at the bottom of the sleeve and this number. Then tie on at the bottom of the sleeve and work around, making decreases (sc2tog) and spreading them out fairly evenly so you end up with the correct stitch count for your wrist. Work a few rows even until the cuff is as long as you like.

LESSON 11: Internal Shaping with a Bust Dart

If you have chosen a size based on shoulder width, but need more room for your bust line, you can use internal shaping to create a bust dart on the two front pieces. For some time now I've been pondering what would be the equivalent of the bust darts used in knitting. The short-row darts that knitters use are impractical for most crocheted items, as it interrupts crochet stitch patterns too visibly.

Here is the solution I've devised for this design: Make Big Pattern Reps (BPR) that have 4 dc rather than 3, and arrange them in the diamond shape of a bust dart on the front pieces. Each BPR measures about ¼"/6mm more than the normal ones (feel free to swatch some BPR to be certain), meaning that for each extra inch/centimeter, you'll need 4 BPR to replace the normal Pattern Repeat (PR). Here's how to determine how many BPR are required across the bust to reach the width you need: The schematic on page 92 shows you the measurement of the front pieces for your size. Compare this number to your actual front bust width to determine how much more fabric you need. Knowing that 4 BPR add an inch/centimeter of fabric, you can now figure out how many of them you need at the bust line.

The BPR will be added gradually, after completing the waist shaping, when you switch back to the larger hook. Add the BPR in an elongated diamond shape over each breast, as shown in figure 1.

Suppose you are making the Large, which measures 10"/25.4cm across each front piece. The two front pieces total 20"/50.8cm but you measure 24"/61cm across your chest. You need 4"/10.2cm extra, or 16 BPR. Each front piece on your size has 10 PR at the bust. In your alteration, on each front piece, you will turn 8 PR into BPR.

To determine the placement of BPR, measure the distance between your waist and the widest part of your bust line. Using row gauge (see Length Alterations, page 37), turn these inches/centimeters into rows. Let's say you have 6 rows between the end of waist shaping and the widest point of your bust. You want to turn PRs into BPRs, beginning on the row after waist shaping. We're going to refer to these 6 bust-shaping rows here and in figure 1 by letters A through F. Since this specific alteration requires an even number of BPR, work 2 BPR at the bottom of the diamond-shaped dart in Row A. If you're working size Large, which has 10 PR on each Front piece, begin with a partial PR as usual and then make 4 PR, then 2 BPR, then another 4 PR in Row A. Work Row B even, working BPR over the BPR in the previous row. On Row C, keep these 2 BPR and work another BPR on either side of them; you now have 4 BPR. To spread the dart out over the available rows, keep Row D the same as Row C. On Row E, keep building your dart by making 2 more BPR—you now have 6 BPR. Make 2 more BPR on Row F (the sixth row of waist-to-bust shaping), and you'll have 8 BPR and all the extra fabric necessary. In the rows after this point, decrease them in the same gradual manner, changing BPR to PR from the outside edges of the dart first. Your decreases should be gradual and can extend over most of the remaining rows on the Front pieces. You needn't decrease on every row. Figure 1 shows how to remove the BPR for size Large.

This strategy can be used on many crochet pieces. Many stitch patterns can accommodate an extra stitch or two, and the enlarged PR will not be noticeable. Experiment with your stitch pattern to find the most elegant solution.

To review, use these steps to create a bust dart:

1. Determine the number of extra inches/centimeters you need.

2. Get a gauge for your BPR by making a swatch, then use that gauge to determine how many total BPR to add.

4. Begin changing PR to BPR right after completing waist shaping, placing them at the center of each Front piece when working two Front pieces. (If you have only one front piece in a different type of sweater, divide it into thirds, mark, and place the darts at the one-third and two-thirds marks. Start by making 1 BPR if your total BPR is an odd number, or 2 if an even number.

5. Add 2 BPR at a time, spreading them out over the rows until you have the full number of BPR at the widest point of the bust.

6. Change BPR back to PR gradually in subsequent rows as you work to the top of the shoulder.

LESSON 12: Widening Sleeves with Internal Shaping

You can use methods similar to those described in Lesson 11 to widen the sleeves of this design.

First determine how many BPR you need at maximum width (at the bicep). Add them gradually, at the start of sleeve shaping. You can add them at regular intervals; for example, if you will need 8 BPR at the bicep, add 4 of them along the forearm and the rest above the elbow (figure 2). Just as in the bust dart, each time you create BPR in a row, they remain in subsequent rows, so that by the time you reach the bicep you have created the desired full width. You can line them up either at the inside or outside of the sleeve, as a V, or you can scatter them more freely in the rows—keep track of how many you need on each row.

You can keep the extra fabric in for the sleeve cap, but be mindful that the sleeve cap doesn't become too large for the armhole (see Lesson 9: Master Class on Armholes and Sleeve Caps, page 88). If you've already finished the armhole on the garment, and it fits, change BPR to PR gradually on the rows of the sleeve cap so that the top of the cap is the same as the original.

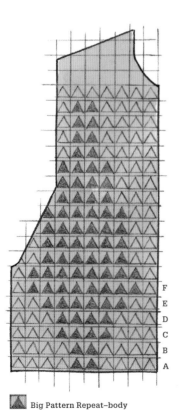

Big Pattern Repeat–body

Figure 1–Bust Dart

Big Pattern Repeat–sleeve

Figure 2–Sleeve

ELEGANZA RAGLAN
raglan pullover construction

This classic design incorporates a few design touches that allow for a better fit, including modifications to the neckline and sleeve.

Stitch Pattern

Ch a multiple of 4 plus 2 + 1 for tch.

Row 1: Sc in 2nd ch from hook, sc in next ch, *dc in next 2 ch, sc in next 2 ch, rep * across, turn.

Row 2: Ch 2 (counts as dc), dc in next sc, *sc in next 2 dc, dc in next 2 sc, rep from *across, ending with dc in next st, hdc in last sc, turn.

Row 3: Ch 1, sc in first hdc, sc in next dc, *dc in next 2 sc, sc in 2 sts, rep from * across, turn.

Rep Rows 2 and 3 for patt.

Note: At the ends of rows, decreases are made by working 2 stitches together to produce a smooth diagonal edge. It's not necessary at the beginnings of rows, where the starting chains naturally form a slanted edge.

Special Notes

1. Count stitches in every dec or inc row.
2. At the beg and ends of rows, the height of dc st is shortened to ch 2 and hdc. In this st patt, the dc sts get pulled down in height, since they are adjacent to sc sts. If no adjustment is made to the sts at the edge, they will stand at their full height, making the edges of the work longer than the rest.
3. Check that the edges or your rows start and end with the same st, counting the last hdc as a dc.
4. On dec sections, the last st in row is 2 sts worked tog to make a smooth edge.
5. After dec or inc, mark the row to facilitate keeping track of the row count.

FINISHED MEASUREMENTS

Bust 34 (37½, 41½, 46, 50)"/86.5 (95, 105.5, 117, 127)cm

MATERIALS AND TOOLS

Classic Elite Premiere (50% Pima cotton, 50% Tencel; 1.75oz/50g = 108 yd/98m): 9 (11, 12, 14, 15) hanks, color 5214 Canary—approx 972 (1188, 1296, 1512, 1620)yds/882 (1078, 1176, 1372, 1470)cm of DK weight yarn; (3)

Crochet hook: 3.75mm (size F-5 U.S.)

Yarn needle

GAUGE

17 sts in patt = 4"/10.2cm; 8 rows = 2½"/6.4cm

Always take time to check your gauge.

Special Abbreviations

sc2tog: [insert hook in next st, yo and draw up a loop] twice, yo, draw yarn through 3 loops.

hdc2tog: [yo, insert hook in next st, yo and draw up a loop,] twice, yo, draw yarn through 5 loops.

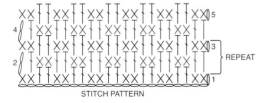

STITCH PATTERN

REPEAT

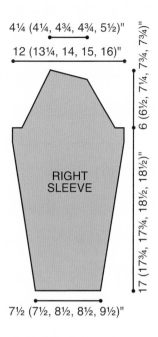

4¼ (4¼, 4¾, 4¾, 5½)"

12 (13¼, 14, 15, 16)"

6 (6½, 7¼, 7¾, 7¾)"

RIGHT SLEEVE

17 (17¾, 17¾, 18½, 18½)"

7½ (7½, 8½, 8½, 9½)"

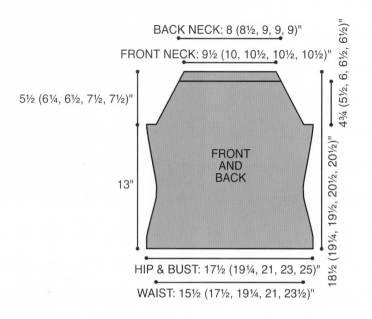

BACK NECK: 8 (8½, 9, 9, 9)"

FRONT NECK: 9½ (10, 10½, 10½, 10½)"

5½ (6¼, 6½, 7½, 7½)"

FRONT AND BACK

13"

4¾ (5½, 6, 6½, 6½)"

18½ (19¼, 19½, 20½, 20½)"

HIP & BUST: 17½ (19¼, 21, 23, 25)"

WAIST: 15½ (17½, 19¼, 21, 23½)"

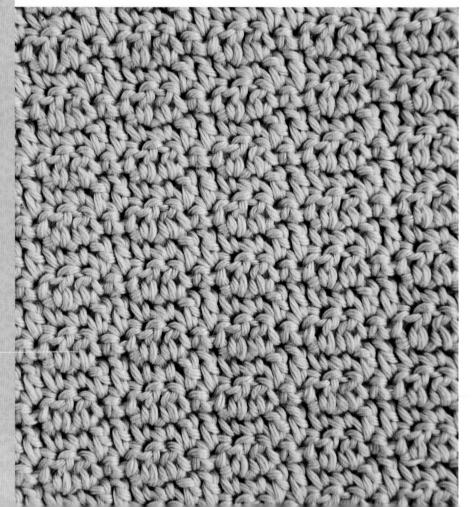

Instructions

Back

Ch 75 (83, 91, 99, 107).

ROWS 1 AND 2: Work in patt across—74, (82, 90, 98, 106) sts.

Hip to Waist Shaping

ROW 3 (DEC ROW): Ch 1, sk first sc, sc in next dc, dc in next 2 sc, cont in patt across to last 2 sts, sc2tog, turn—72 (80, 88, 96, 104) sts.

ROW 4: Ch 2, sc in next 2 dc, cont in patt across, hdc in last sc, turn.

ROW 5: Ch 1, sc in first hdc, dc in next 2 sc, cont in patt across, sc in tch, turn.

ROW 6: Rep row 4.

ROW 7 (DEC ROW): Ch 1, sk first hdc, dc in next 2 sc, cont in patt across to last 2 sts, hdc2tog, turn—70 (78, 86, 94, 102) sts.

ROW 8: Ch 1, sc in first 2 sts, cont in patt across, ending with sc in last 2 sts.

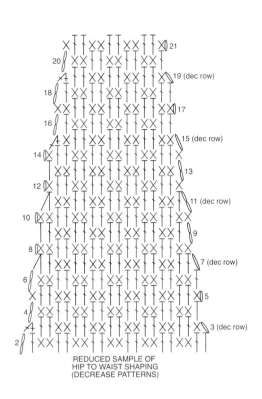

REDUCED SAMPLE OF
HIP TO WAIST SHAPING
(DECREASE PATTERNS)

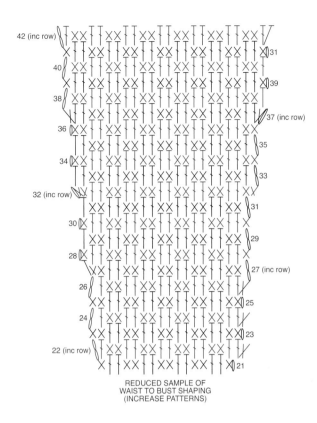

REDUCED SAMPLE OF
WAIST TO BUST SHAPING
(INCREASE PATTERNS)

ROW 9: Ch 2, work in patt across.

ROW 10: Rep row 8.

ROW 11 (DEC ROW): Ch 2, dc in next sc (counts as dc2tog), sc in next 2 sts, cont in patt across, hdc2tog over last 2 sc, turn—68 (76, 84, 92, 100) sts.

ROW 12: Ch 1, sc in first hdc, dc in next 2 sc, cont in patt across, sc in tch, turn.

ROW 13: Ch 2, sc in next 2 dc, cont in patt across, ending with hdc in last sc, turn.

ROW 14: Rep row 12.

ROW 15 (DEC ROW): Ch 1, sk first sc, sc in next 2 dc, cont in patt across to last 2 sts, sc2tog over last 2 sts—66 (74, 82, 90, 98) sts.

ROWS 16–18: Work even in patt.

ROW 19 (DEC ROW): Rep Row 3—64 (72, 80, 88, 96) sts.

ROWS 20 AND 21: Work even in patt.

Waist to Bust Shaping

ROWS 22—42: Inc 1 st at each end in this row, and every 5th row thereafter until 74 (82, 90, 98, 106) sts are on work.

Raglan Shaping

ROW 1: Ch 1, sl st over first 4 (5, 6, 8, 9) sts, starting in same st, work in patt across to last 3 (4, 5, 7, 8) sts, turn, leaving rem sts unworked—68 (74, 80, 84, 90) sts.

ROWS 2—18 (20, 21, 23, 27): Work 14 (16, 18, 20, 23) rows, dec 1 st at each end on every row, ending with 34 (36, 38, 38, 38) sts.

Front

Work same as Back through Row 15 (17, 19, 20, 24—40 (42, 44, 44, 44) sts at end of last row. Fasten off.

Right Sleeve

Note: It's easy to lose count on these rows, especially where the tch is a ch-2—they tend to almost disappear. Be sure to check your stitch count at every increase row to stay on track.

Ch 33 (33, 37, 37, 41).

ROW 1: Sc in 2nd ch from hook, *dc in next 2 ch, sc in next 2 ch, rep from * across to last 3 ch, dc in next 2 ch, sc in last ch, turn—32 (32, 36, 36, 40) sts.

ROWS 2—55 (57, 57, 59, 59): Inc 1 st at each end of every 4th (4th, 4th, 3rd, 3rd) row [8 (11, 11, 5, 5) times]; then inc 1 st at each end of every 5th (5th, 5th, 5th, 4th, 4th) row [3 (1, 1, 9, 9) times]; then work 7 rows even in patt—54 (56, 60, 64, 68) sts.

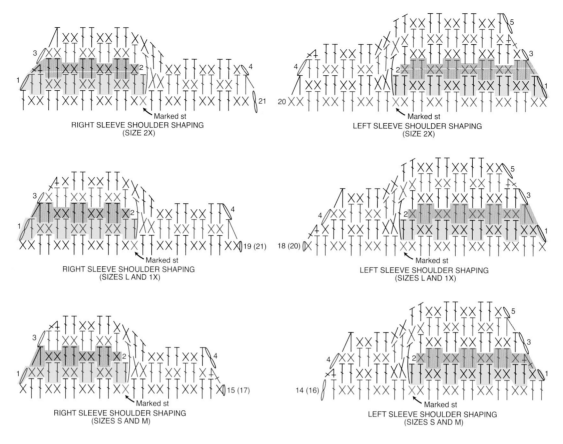

RIGHT SLEEVE SHOULDER SHAPING
(SIZE 2X)

LEFT SLEEVE SHOULDER SHAPING
(SIZE 2X)

RIGHT SLEEVE SHOULDER SHAPING
(SIZES L AND 1X)

LEFT SLEEVE SHOULDER SHAPING
(SIZES L AND 1X)

RIGHT SLEEVE SHOULDER SHAPING
(SIZES S AND M)

LEFT SLEEVE SHOULDER SHAPING
(SIZES S AND M)

NOTE: The stitch that extends over the two short rows should be made normal size to eliminate gaps. The top of sleeve cap will be a straight diagonal.

Shape Cap

ROW 1: Ch 1, sl st over first 4 (5, 6, 8, 9) sts, starting in same st, work in patt across to last 3 (4, 5, 7, 8) sts, leaving rem sts unworked—46 (48, 50, 50, 52) sts.

ROWS 2—15 (17, 19, 21, 21): Dec 1 st at each end of next 10 (8, 6, 4, 4) rows; then dec 1 st at each end of every other row 2 (4, 4, 8, 8) times—24 (24, 26, 26, 28) sts at end of last row.

Shoulder Shaping (short rows)

ROW 1: Dec 1 st at beg of row, work in patt for 11 (11, 12, 12, 13) more sts, mark st on prev row where last st was worked, turn, leaving rem sts unworked—12 (12, 13, 13, 14) sts.

ROW 2: Do not ch 1, sk first st, work in patt across to last 2 sts, dec 1 st in last 2 sts in patt, turn—10 (10, 11, 11, 12) sts.

ROW 3: Dec 1 at beg of row, work in patt to end of row, work next st in patt in marked st 3 rows below (pull this stitch snug to prevent a gap), cont in patt across next 9 (9, 10, 10, 11) sts of last row before short rows, dec 1 st in last 2 sts—20 (20, 22, 22, 24) sts.

ROW 4: Work in patt, dec 1 at each end of row—18 (18, 20, 20, 22) sts. Fasten off.

Left Sleeve

Note: In order for short rows to begin at back of Sleeve, shoulder shaping begins one row sooner than on Right Sleeve.

Work same as right Sleeve through Row 14 (16, 18, 20, 20) of shape cap—26 (26, 28, 28, 30) sts.

Shoulder Shaping (short rows)

ROW 1: Dec 1 st at beg of row, work in patt for 14 (14, 15, 15, 16) more sts, mark st on prev row where last st was worked, turn, leaving rem sts unworked—15 (15, 16, 16, 17) sts.

ROW 2: Do not ch 1, sk first st, work in patt across to last 2 sts, dec 1 st in last 2 sts in patt, turn—13 (13, 14, 14, 15) sts.

ROW 3: Dec 1 at beg of row, work in patt to end of row, work next st in patt in marked st 3 rows below (pull this stitch snug to prevent a gap), cont in patt across next 8 (8, 9, 9, 10) sts of last row before short rows, dec 1 st in last 2 sts—22 (22, 24, 24, 26) sts.

ROW 4: Work in patt, dec 1 at each end of row—20 (20, 22, 22, 24) sts. Fasten off.

ROW 5: Rep row 4—18 (18, 20, 20, 22). Fasten off.

Finishing

Sew side seams. Sew sleeve to raglan seams. Sew Sleeve seams.

Neck Edging

RND 1: With RS facing, join yarn on top right back in st next to the raglan "seam," ch 1, sc in each st around neck opening, working 34 (36, 38, 38, 38) sc across back, 18 (18, 20, 20, 22, 24) across each Sleeve, 40 (42, 44, 44, 44) across Fronts, sl st in first sc to join—110 (114, 122, 126, 130) sts. Note: If you need an extra st at seams to avoid gaps, you may add them.

RND 2: Ch 1, *sc in next 2 sc, sc2tog in next 2 sts, rep from * around, ending with sc in each of last 3 (2, 0, 3, 2) sts—83 (86, 92, 95, 98) sts.

RND 3: Ch 2, (yo, pick up loop in next st) 2 times, yo, pick up loop in same st as last lp, yo, draw through 7 loops on hook (cluster made), *yo, pick up loop in same st as last lp, yo, pick up lp in next st, yo, pick up lp in same st, yo, draw through 7 lps on hook, rep from * around, sl st to top of beg ch-2. Fasten off.

THE ELEGANZA RAGLAN IS an easygoing, versatile sweater with a textured stitch at the neckline that adds the elegance. Worked in pieces from the bottom, it is just like any typical bottom-up sweater until it arrives at the armholes. Everything you've already learned about torso length and waist shaping will also apply to the raglan sweater.

The differences begin after the armhole, which is simpler on raglans than on set-in sleeves. Raglans have diagonal seams running from the neckline to the bottom of the armhole. Not all raglan seams are straight diagonals, and many interesting designs can be created by playing with variations.

Construction Details

This simple raglan has a few neat adjustments that make the fit especially nice. A raglan sits more properly on the neckline if the back neck is higher than the front. In this design, we work more rows on the back piece to achieve this result. Consequently, there needs to be an adjustment in the sleeve as well. In order for the raglan sleeve to match both front and back, one side of the sleeve cap—the side that will be sewn to the back—is longer than the other. That is accomplished by adding 3 short rows at the top of the sleeve. The top of the sleeve will be slightly angled, but that won't be visible when the pieces are sewn together.

Fit and Choosing Your Size

Rather than being super-snug, this sweater offers relaxed fit at the bust and sleeve. The raglan armhole is less fitted than a set-in sleeve, so there is built-in ease. Pick the size that works best for your bust and sleeve widths (including the amount of ease you like in the final measurements) based on the schematic. Waist shaping can be eliminated or altered on this design as we've shown on other sweaters.

Choosing Yarn

Use any worsted-weight yarn with good drape. I love it in the soft Pima cotton used here, but a wool or wool blend can work just as well. If you would like something that's washable, use a high-quality acrylic or bamboo.

LESSON 13: Master Class in Sleeve Alteration

This is the only project in *Custom Crocheted Sweaters* with long sleeves, so it's perfect for an in-depth look at sleeve alteration. Increasing or decreasing stitches in this pattern is simple, so you can tailor your results quite precisely.

Most sleeve alterations are concerned with achieving the proper measurement at the bicep, or upper arm. Think about where on the upper arm you want to reach the full width. For some people that fullness extends almost to the elbow, for some a little higher. The first step, in order to calculate properly, is to measure the distance from the wrist to where the full part of your arm begins. You want to get to the necessary stitch count here—not higher—to avoid a tight sleeve.

LENGTHENING THE SLEEVE

Suppose you are making the largest size, which has a sleeve length of 18½"/47cm, measured from the wrist to where the raglan shaping begins. Is that the proper measurement for your sleeve length? If not, let's start by figuring out how to adjust the number of rows so they work out to the right length. Consult your measurements to determine your actual sleeve length from underarm. Let's suppose it should be 17"/43.2cm instead of 18½"/47cm.

Gauge is 17 st in patt =

4"/10.2cm; 8 rows = 2½"/6.4cm.

Calculate the number of rows by dividing your target inches/centimeters number by the inches/centimeters side of the row gauge equation. (For a refresher on row gauge, see Shaping and Alteration 101, page 34).

$$17"/43.2cm \div 2\frac{1}{2}" = 6.8$$

6.8 x 8 rows = 54.4 rows

You can decide whether to make 54 rows and have it be a bit shorter, or 55 and a bit longer. No big deal either way.

Next, determine the distance from your wrist to where you want the widest part to be. On someone whose arm is at full width 2"/5cm above the elbow, the measurement from wrist to that point might be around 12"/30.5cm; when altering, you'll need your exact measurement of course.

$$12"/30.5cm \div 2\frac{1}{2}"/6.4cm = 4.8$$

4.8 x 8 rows = 38.4 rows

Rounding that down to 38, we know the sleeve should be at its fullest width by the 38th row on the sleeve.

If you're sticking with the same sleeve width and only changing the shaping, check the number of increase rows on the pattern for your size. We're not concerned with row number, only how many increases are needed. The second row of Right Sleeve instructions gives us the information needed:

ROWS 2–55 (57, 57, 59, 59): Inc 1 st at each end of every 4th (4th, 4th, 3rd, 3rd) row [8 (11, 11, 5, 5) times]; then inc 1 st at each end of every 5th (5th, 5th, 5th, 4th, 4th) row [3 (1, 1, 9, 9) times]; then work 7 rows even in patt—54 (56, 60, 64, 68) sts.

The directions tell us that for the largest size, there are 5 increases, then 9 increases, a total of 14 rows on which 2-stitch increases are made. You will make the same number of increases on your sleeve, but they will be closer together instead of spread out as they are in the original instructions. In other words, you are making the rate of increase faster.

Knowing that you have to make 14 increases within 38 rows of shaping, you calculate as follows:

38 rows ÷ 14 increase rows = 2.714

Oh dear, a fraction! Well, that means that sometimes you'll increase on every 2nd row, sometimes on every third. Here's a simple way to figure out what to do.

$$14\overline{)38} \quad \begin{array}{r} 2 \\ \underline{28} \\ 10 \end{array}$$

That means if I increased every 2 rows, I would be done with all the shaping on the 28th row instead of the 38th, leaving 10 rows extra. To get the shaping to end where I want, I'm going to have one more row between increases 10 times. Since there are 14 increases altogether, I will make 4 of them 2 rows apart and 10 of them 3 rows apart. To make the taper as even as possible, intersperse the more rapid increases between the slower increases, as follows: increase on rows 2, 5, 8, 10, 13, 16, 19, 21, 24, 27, 30, 32, 35, and 38.

You can use this procedure whenever your total row number for shaping is not evenly divisible by the number of increase rows. Divide the total number of shaping rows by the number of increase rows. Ignore the remainder for the moment, and figure on increasing at the rate shown by your answer (2 in the example above) a certain number of times. The remainder tells you how many times to have another row between increases (10 in the example)—that's how many times you'll increase at the slower rate (every third row in the example). Subtract this number from the number of increase rows. The answer tells you how many times you'll increase at the faster rate (every second row).

To summarize, here are the steps necessary for altering sleeve length:

1. Refer to your measurement from armhole to bottom of sleeve.

2. Use gauge to figure out how many rows to add or remove from the pattern.

3. Determine where you want shaping to end on the sleeve—where your arm is widest.

4. Compute the distance from the bottom of the sleeve to where shaping ends.

5. Use row gauge to figure out how many rows this requires.

6. Review the pattern to see how many increase rows it has.

7. Divide the number of shaping rows by the number of increase rows. The resulting number is how many rows between increases. If it's a fraction, follow the procedure above to evenly spread out your increase rows.

Widening the Sleeve

Suppose the sleeve width of 16"/40.6cm is not enough and you need 2"/5cm more ease, for comfort, for a total width of 18"/45.7cm. How many stitches will that require? Divide the target number of inches/centimeters by the inches/centimeters side of the stitch gauge equation:

$$18"/45.7cm \div 4"/10.2cm = 4.5$$

$$4.5 \times 17 \text{ stitches} = 76.5 \text{ stitches}$$

A fraction of a stitch is not significant, so we will aim for 76 stitches. Now let's see how many stitches overall must change from the beginning of sleeve shaping to the end.

Take the number of stitches at the bicep and subtract the number of stitches at the wrist:

$$76 - 41 = 35$$

Since stitches will be added on both sides of the sleeve, divide this number in half to find out how many increase rows you will need. Since we got an odd number, I'm going to take back that extra half stitch I tossed out earlier and round the stitch number up to 77:

$$77 - 41 = 36$$

That means 18 increases, adding 1 stitch on each side, will occur. We want to distribute these increases as evenly as possible over the 35 rows.

35 ÷ 18—whoa, this is going to be complicated!—couldn't I go back and round that row number up to 36? Sure! We're talking very minimal distance with this row gauge, so it's fine.

36 shaping rows ÷ 18 increase rows = 2

This means that you will increase every other row. Beginning with the stitch count for the largest size, start increasing on row 2, and increase every even row up to and including row 36, for a total stitch count of 77. Write out all the row counts before actually stitching, just to be sure.

When you are altering a sleeve for width, follow the first five steps summarized above for length. Here is a new step 6:

6. Determine the number of stitches to increase overall. Divide this number by 2 to determine how many increase rows you need.

This works if the increases are in fact made 2 stitches at a time, which is often the case. If more than 2 stitches are increased per row, divide the number of stitches to be added by the number of stitches per increase. The answer tells you how many increase rows you need.

You can now continue to step 7, dividing the number of shaping rows by the number of increase rows to find out how many rows between increases.

You can use this method to alter any sleeve. Keep in mind that when you alter sleeve width, it will affect the finished dimension of the cap as well. On a raglan design, a longer cap will make the neckline larger. If that doesn't suit you, you can decrease more stitches as you work the cap to arrive at the correct stitch count at the top. The caps on this pattern have 1 stitch removed at each end on every row, but you can remove 2 stitches on each end here and there. Remember that the number of rows in the cap must match the number of rows in the raglan armhole, as they will be sewn together. On a raglan, unlike in fitted sleeves, these must match very closely.

On a set-in sleeve cap, the number of stitches added will have to be subtracted as you work the cap of the sleeve to get to the proper measurements at the top of the sleeve cap. To review alteration strategies for set-in sleeves, see Lesson 9: Master Class on Armholes and Sleeve Caps, page 88.

UPTOWN
top-down construction

This top-down raglan features a small stitch pattern that creates an interesting fabric with bold vertical lines.

Stitch Pattern

Pattern repeat (patt rep) = (sc, ch 2, sc) in same st or space.

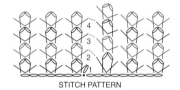

STITCH PATTERN

Special Notes

1. This pattern requires two rounds to create an increase of one pattern rep. To stay on track, the increase points are marked on each round. The rounds begin at the center back of the garment.

2. It's tempting to skip the placing and moving of markers on each round, but don't give in! It's way too easy to miscount a pattern rep, especially with this stitch pattern, and before you know it, your whole pattern is off. Be diligent about moving your markers on each round.

FINISHED MEASUREMENTS
Bust 34 (37½, 40, 42½, 46, 50)"/86.5 (95, 101.5, 108, 117, 127)cm

MATERIALS AND TOOLS
Lorna's Laces Honor (70% baby alpaca, 30% silk, 3.5oz/100g = 275 yd/248m): 6 (7, 8, 9, 10, 11) balls, color Growth— approx 1650 (1925, 2200, 2475, 2750, 3025)yds/1488 (1736, 1984, 2232, 2480, 2728)m of DK weight yarn; (3)

Crochet hooks: 4.00 mm (size G-6 U.S.); 3.75 mm (size F-5 U.S.)—for neck edging

Yarn needle

GAUGE
With G hook, 4 patt reps = 2 1/2"/6.4cm; 8 rows in patt = 2"/5cm

Always take time to check your gauge.

Special Abbreviations

inc 1: Sc in next sc, patt rep in next ch-2 sp, sc in next sc.

inc 2: Patt rep in sc, patt rep in next ch-2 sp, sk sc, patt rep in next sc.

inc 3: (Sc, ch 2, sc, ch 2, sc) in designated st.

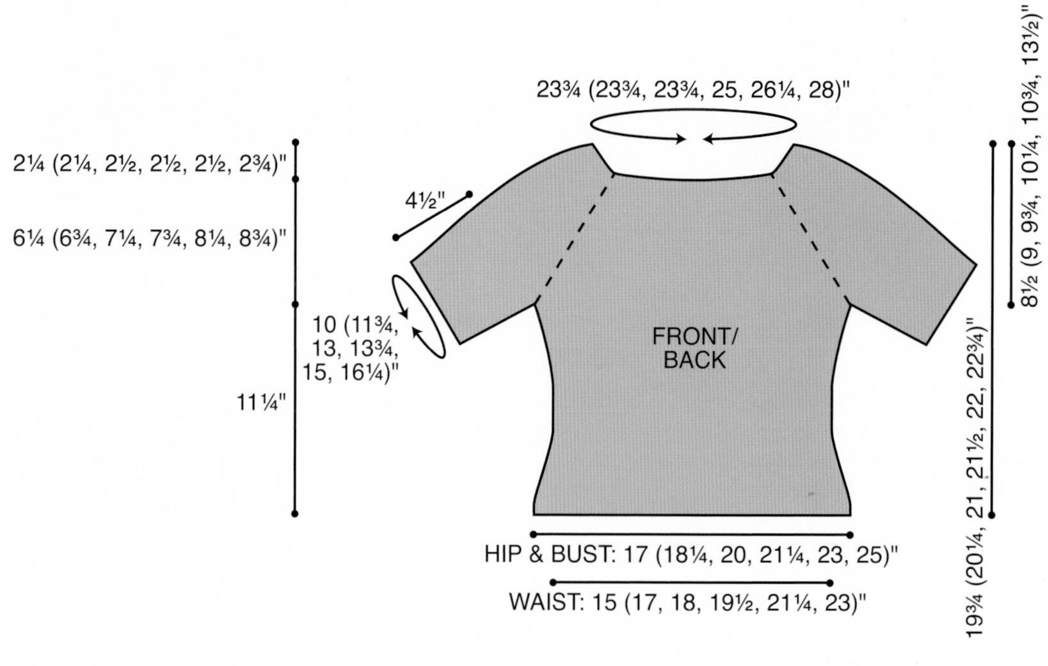
23¾ (23¾, 23¾, 25, 26¼, 28)"
2¼ (2¼, 2½, 2½, 2½, 2¾)"
4½"
6¼ (6¾, 7¼, 7¾, 8¼, 8¾)"
10 (11¾, 13, 13¾, 15, 16¼)"
11¼"
FRONT/ BACK
HIP & BUST: 17 (18¼, 20, 21¼, 23, 25)"
WAIST: 15 (17, 18, 19½, 21¼, 23)"
8½ (9, 9¾, 10¼, 10¾, 13½)"
19¾ (20¼, 21, 21½, 22, 22¾)"

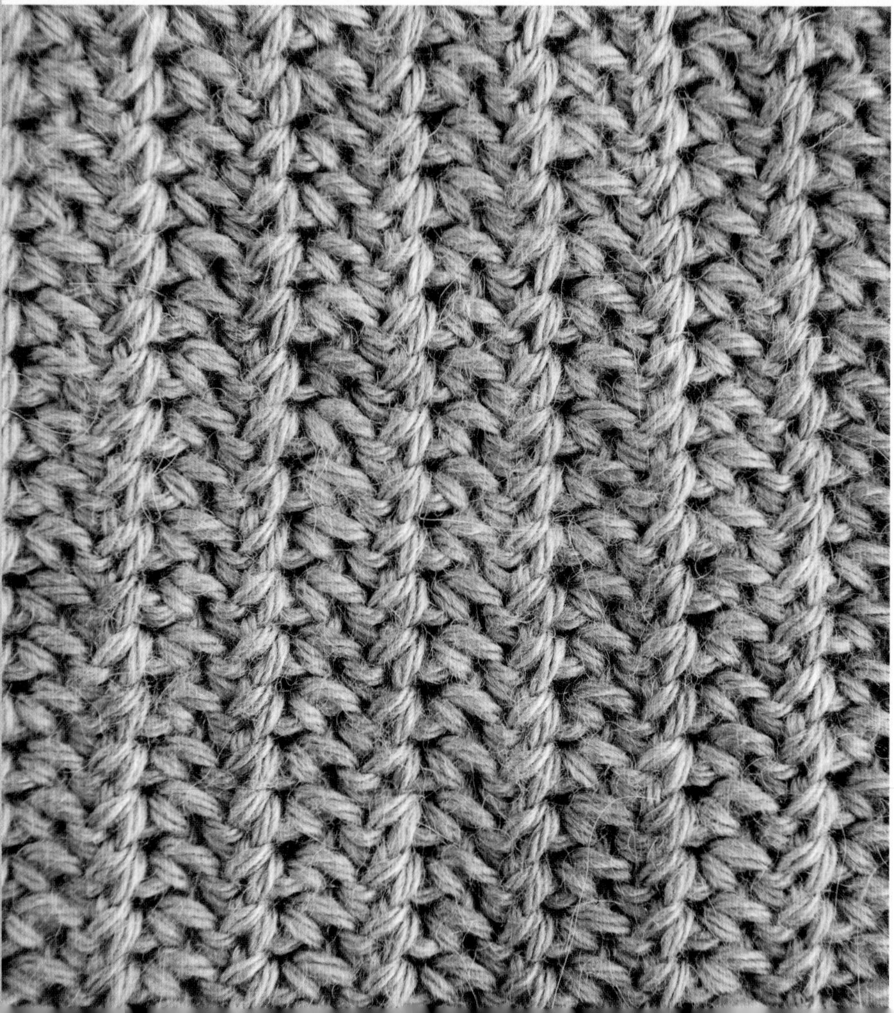

Instructions

Yoke

With G hook, ch 114 (114, 114, 117, 126, 132) and being careful not to twist ch, sl st to first ch to join.

RND 1: Ch 1, *(sc, ch 2, sc) in first ch, sk next 2 ch, rep from * 37 (37, 37, 39, 41, 44) times. From beg, count 6 (6, 6, 6, 7, 7) patt reps and PM in first sc of last patt rep, count 7 (7, 7, 8, 8, 9) patt reps and PM in last patt rep made, count 12 (12, 12, 12, 13, 13) patt rep and PM in last patt rep made, count 7 (7, 7, 8, 8, 9) patt rep and PM in last patt rep made, 6 patt reps rem—38 (38, 38, 40, 42, 44) patt reps; 11 (11, 11, 11, 12, 12) patt reps on front and back, 6 (6, 6, 7, 7, 8) patt reps on each sleeve, plus 4 corner patt reps. PM at end of rnd. Cont working in spiral without joining. Note that rounds begin on the back of garment.

RND 2 (INC 1 RND): Starting in first ch-2 sp, (sc, ch-2, sc) in each ch-2 sp to marked patt rep, Inc 1, rep from * 3 times, (sc, ch-2, sc) in each ch-2 sp to end marker. Move markers to first sc of Inc 1 at each corner; move marker up to last sc at end of rnd.

RND 3 (INC 2 RND): Starting in first ch-2 sp, *(sc, ch-2, sc) in each ch-2 sp to next corner marker, Inc 2, rep from * 3 times, (sc, ch-2, sc) in each ch-2 sp to end marker—46 (46, 46, 48, 50, 54) patt reps; 13 (13, 13, 13, 14, 14) patt reps on front and back; 8 (8, 8, 9, 9, 10) patt reps on each sleeve, plus 4 corner patt reps. Move markers to center ch-2 space of each corner; move marker up to last sc at end of rnd and continue to do so throughout Yoke.

RNDS 4 AND 5 (EVEN): (Sc, ch-2, sc) in each ch-2 sp around.

Size S only:

RNDS 6–21: Rep Rnds 2–5 (4 times—78 patt reps; 21 patt reps on front and back (body), 16 patt reps on each sleeve plus 4 corners. Move markers to center ch-2 space of each corner; move marker up to last sc at end of rnd.

Note: Next 2 rnds define the technique of working 2 inc on front and back (body), but no inc on sleeves.

RND 22: Starting in first ch-2 sp, *(sc, ch-2, sc) in each ch-2 sp to first sc of next marked corner, sc in first sc of corner, (sc, ch-2, sc) in marked corner ch-2 sp, sk next sc, (sc, ch 2, sc) in each ch-2 sp to next marked corner, (sc, ch-2, sc) in marked corner ch-2 sp, sc in next sc of corner, rep from * once, (sc, ch-2, sc) in each ch-2 sp to end.

RND 23: Starting in first ch-2 sp, *(sc, ch-2, sc) in each ch-2 sp to first sc of next marked corner, (sc, ch 2, sc) in added sc before corner, (sc, ch-2, sc) in corner ch-2 sp, (sc, ch 2, sc) in each ch-2 sp to next marked corner, (sc, ch-2, sc) in corner ch-2 sp, sk next sc, (sc, ch 2, sc) in next added sc, rep from * once, (sc, ch-2, sc) in each ch-2 sp to end marker—82 patt reps; 23 body/16 sleeves plus 4 corners.

RNDS 24 AND 25: Rep Rows 22 and 23—86 patt reps; 25 body/16 sleeves plus 4 corners.

Size M only:

RNDS 6–23: Rep Rnds 2–5 (4 times); rep rnds 2-3 (once—82 patt reps; 22 body/17 sleeves plus 4 corners at end of last rnd.

RNDS 24–27: Rep Rnds 22 and 23 of size S (twice—94 patt reps; 27 body/18 sleeves plus 4 corners. Continue to Body.

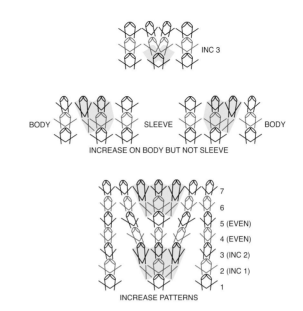

Size L only:
RNDS 6–29: Rep Rnds 2–5 (6 times); rep Rnds 2–3 (once—104 patt reps; 29 body/20 sleeves plus 4 corners. Continue to Body.

Size 1X only:
RND 6–27: Rep Rnds 2–5 (5 times); rep Rnds 2–3 (once—100 patt reps; 27 body/21 sleeves plus 4 corners.

RNDS 26–29: Rep Rnds 22 and 23 of size S (twice—108 patt reps; 31 body/21 sleeves plus 4 corners. Continue to Body.

Size 2X only:
RNDS 6–27: Rep Rnds 2-5 (4 times), rep rnds 2–3 (once—106 patt reps; 28 body/23 sleeves plus 4 corners.

RNDS 28–33: Rep Rnds 22 and 23 of size S (3 times—118 patt reps; 34 body/23 sleeves at end of last row plus 4 corners. Continue to Body.

Size 3X only:
RNDS 6–27: Rep Rnds 2-5 (4 times), rep Rnds 2–3 (once—108 patt reps; 28 body/24 sleeves plus 4 corners.

RNDS 28–35: Rep Rnds 22 and 23 of size S (4 times—124 patt reps; 36 body/24 sleeves at end of last row plus 4 corners. Continue to Body.

Note: Try on sweater to determine if you need to add length to yoke before beginning body.

Body

86 (94, 104, 108, 118, 124) patt reps.
Note: Next rnd will add sts for underarm.

RND 1 (JOINING RND): *Work even in patt to next marker, *sc in marked ch-2 sp, ch 6 (9, 9, 9, 9, 12), sk next 16 (18, 20, 21, 23, 24) patt reps for sleeve, sc in next marked ch-2 sp, work in patt across to next M, rep from * once. Remove corner markers.

RND 2: Work even in patt to underarm ch, *sk next ch, (sc, ch 2, sc) in next ch, [sk next 2 ch, (sc, ch 2, sc) in next ch] 1 (2, 2, 2, 2, 3) times, sk next ch*, work in patt across to next underarm ch, rep from * to * once, work in patt to end of rnd—54 (60, 64, 68, 74, 80) patt reps.

Note: There are 2 (3, 3, 3, 3, 4) pattern repeats at each underarm. PM in 1st (2nd, 2nd, 2nd, 2nd, 2nd) ch-2 sp on each underarm. When making 2nd rnd of decreases, work the sc just before and just after the skipped sc tightly, to avoid a gap over skipped sc.

Torso Shaping

RNDS 3–6: Work even in patt.
RND 7: *Work even in patt to marker, sc in marked sp, move marker up to sc just made, rep from * once, work in patt to end—52 (58, 62, 66, 72, 78) patt reps plus 2 sc.
RND 8: *Work even to marker, PM in patt rep just made, sk marked sc, rep from * once, work in patt to end—52 (58, 62, 66, 72, 78) patt reps.
RNDS 9–15: Work even in patt, moving markers up as work progresses.
RND 16: Rep Rnd 7—50 (56, 60, 64, 70, 76) patt reps.
RND 17: *Work even in patt to M, sk marked sc, patt rep in next ch-2 sp, PM in same patt rep, rep from * once, work in patt to end.
RNDS 18–22: Work even in patt, moving markers up as work progresses.
RNDS 23 AND 24: Rep Rnds 7 and 8—(54, 58, 62, 68, 74) patt reps.
RNDS 24–28: Work even in patt for 5 rows or to desired length for bottom of waist.

Hip Shaping

RND 29: *Work even to marker, Inc 3 in marked ch-2 sp, PM in 2nd sp of inc, rep from * once, work in patt to end—50 (56, 60, 64, 70, 76) patt reps.
RND 30: Work even in patt, working patt rep in each ch-2 sp of inc.
RNDS 31–35: Work even in patt, moving markers up as work progresses.
RND 36: *Work even to marker, Inc 3 in marked ch-2 sp, PM in 1st sp of inc, rep from * once, work in patt to end—52 (58, 62, 66, 72, 78) patt reps.
RND 37: Work even in patt, working patt rep in each ch-2 sp of inc.
RNDS 38–43: Work even in patt, moving markers up as work progresses.
RND 44 AND 45: Rep Rnds 29 and 30—54 (60, 64, 68, 74, 80) patt reps.
OPTIONAL: Continue to work even in patt until desired length. If you make the sweater long enough to reach the widest part of your hips, you may need to do an additional inc. Place the inc in marked sp.
At end of last rnd, sl st in next sc to join.
Fasten off.
Note: If you haven't been marking the end of the rnd, it can be found from the top of the garment, where you should be able to see the beginning of the first round. Follow the vertical line formed by the pattern until you get to the garment's bottom.

Sleeves

Note: You will be adding rows to the sleeves. Before you begin, take a good look at the underarm of the sleeve and the sts on either side of it. You will be working into foundation ch at the base of each patt rep at the underarm. Notice that just above the underarm section, and before the next patt rep on the sleeve, there is one sc just before underarm sts are added. Work one patt rep into these sc on both the front and back to eliminate any unsightly holes between Body and Sleeve. For the same reason, close the first round of Sleeve with a slip st, but not subsequent rnds.

RND 1: With G hook, and with RS facing, join yarn in chain at base of first patt rep at the underarm, ch 1, work (sc, ch 2, sc) in base ch of same patt rep, [sk next 2 ch, (sc, ch 2, sc) in next ch] 1 (2, 2, 2, 2, 3) times, PM in 1st (2nd, 2nd, 2nd, 2nd, 2nd) ch-2 sp of underarm, work (sc, ch 2, sc) in side of next sc (as explained above), work in patt around entire sleeve, work (sc, ch 2, sc) in next sc (as explained above), sl st in first sc to join—18 (21, 23, 24, 26, 28) patt reps.

RND 2: Work even in patt around, do not sl st at end of rnd, but work in spiral as on body.

RND 3: Work in patt to marker, sc in marked sp, work in patt to end—17 (20, 22, 23, 25, 27) patt reps.

RND 4: Work in patt around, sk marked sc, PM in patt rep just made, cont in patt to end.

RNDS 5–10: Work even in patt around.

RNDS 11 AND 12: Rep rnds 3 and 4.

RNDS 13–18: Work even in patt around.

OPTIONAL: To make sleeves longer, repeat last 8 rows to desired length.

Note: Each dec of 1 patt rep removes about 1/2"/1.3cm of width. At end of last round, slip st in next sc to join. Fasten off.

Rep Sleeve in other sleeve opening.

Finishing

Use one hook size smaller than what you used for the garment. This will make a firm, subtle edge that draws in the neckline slightly.

With F hook, join yarn on neck opening, at top of raglan "seam."

RND 1: Ch 1, working across foundation ch, sc in each ch around.

RND 2: Sl st in each sc around. Fasten off.

UPTOWN IS A SPORTY, everyday item that can work with slacks or a skirt. I found a simple pattern stitch that creates nice drape and has a strong vertical element, to show off the internal raglan shaping. The alpaca content of the yarn makes the sweater hug the body very nicely and feels like a dream on the skin.

Construction Details

As explained in the Overview of Sweater Construction (page 10), top-down sweaters often begin by working the entire circumference of the neckline, which is then divided at four corners where increases are made. Those four points delineate the front, back, and sleeves of the garment. By adding stitches as you progress, you are enlarging the size of the body and the sleeves at the same time. After completing the yoke, the body is worked separately from the sleeves. In crochet, this is incredibly easy, compared to knitting, since no stitches need to be moved off needles. You simply skip the stitches of the sleeve on the first round after the yoke is complete. On that same round, you also add underarm stitches, between ½" and 2"/1.3 and 5cm on each side, depending on your size.

From this point you continue working the sweater down over the torso, adding waist shaping and working to whatever length is desired. After the torso section is done, you tie on at the sleeves and taper them down to their finished lengths.

Substituting Yarn

Again, a yarn with good drape will give you best results for this sweater. Use a soft DK weight yarn, and swatch first to see how the choice of yarn affects this stitch pattern. You don't want the ch-2 space in the stitch pattern to make visible holes in the garment, and the fuzzy alpaca used here accomplishes this.

Fit and Choosing Your Size

This sweater can have a snug or relaxed fit at the bust and sleeves. Choose the size based on the bust width measurement given on the schematic.

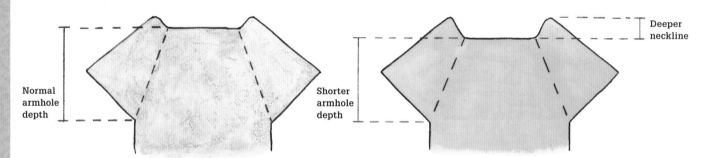

The original neckline is at left. Note that extra PR on each sleeve create the deeper neckline and shorter armhole depth at the right.

Figure 1

LESSON 14: Adding Neckline Depth

Deep necklines are attractive on many people, and are especially flattering to those with large upper bodies. In top-down construction, we lower the neckline by increasing its circumference, adding more stitches to the portion of the neckline that is at the top of the sleeve. That way, the neckline drops lower but does not get wider (see figure 1).

When lowering a neckline, you must take into account that half of the extra fabric lands on the front and half on the back. If you want the neckline to sit 1"/2.5cm lower, you'll add 2"/5cm at the top of each sleeve. To compensate for the deeper neckline, your yoke can be 1"/2.5cm shorter. For convenience, let's plot out an alteration that fits nicely into the gauge. Since 4 PR = 2½"/6.4cm, let's examine how you'd make the neckline 1¼"/3.2cm deeper.

To make this alteration, add 4 Pattern Repeats (PR) on each sleeve, for a total of 8 more PR. The 8 PR are added in the very first round, so you will need 24 extra chains to begin the pattern, 3 chains for each PR. After completing Round 1 of the pattern, you will have a PR count that is 8 more than what is in the pattern. To insure that the extra PR are placed over the sleeves and not over the front or back, follow this procedure carefully:

Place your first marker as indicated in the pattern. Before placing your second marker, count out the number of PR in the pattern for your size, plus an additional 4 PR. You have now added 4 PR to one sleeve. The third marker should be placed as written in the pattern. For the fourth marker, count out the number of PR indicated in the pattern, plus an additional 4 PR. You have now added 4 PR to the second sleeve.

This approach will add depth to the neckline, but not width. Since the sweater will begin 1¼"/3.2cm lower on the body, you will work fewer rows from the neckline to the bottom of the yoke. To adjust for this difference, work 4 fewer rows than indicated for your size between the first and last round of the yoke. This, in turn, will affect the rate of increase, so that you will have the correct PR counts at the end of the yoke. Check the pattern carefully at the end of the yoke for the correct PR counts for your front, back, and sleeves. Since you began with 4 additional PR on each sleeve, you can skip the first sleeve increases and begin them where the PR count in the pattern matches your PR count. For the bust, you may need to add increases on rounds 4 and 5—to the front and back only— to achieve the correct count. If necessary, you can add a few more rounds to arrive at the correct PR count. This will add to the armhole depth, but at our gauge: 8 rows = 2"/5cm, that's not significant. This type of sweater works fine with a deep armhole.

All the alterations possible with other sweater constructions can be done for top-down garments. The sweater's length can be altered, as can the waist shaping and sleeve length. Refer to Shaping and Alteration 101 (page 34) and other relevant lessons for these alterations.

SHRUG HUG
top-down construction variation

Love sock yarn? You can use it in this adorable little sweater.

Special Stitches

Mini Ripple: 3 dc in next st, Dc3tog.

V: (Dc, ch 1, dc) in indicated st

Dc3tog: [Yo, insert hook in next st, yo and draw up a loop, yo, draw yarn through 2 loops] 3 times, yo, draw yarn through 4 loops.

Note: Always work over next 3 sts.

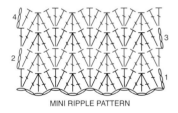

MINI RIPPLE PATTERN

Special Notes

1. Working into V means working under ch-1 sp of V.
2. Be sure that when you start the ripples section on each side of your rectangle, they start and end with 2 dc, not 3. As you progress from one row to the next, you will be adding single dc's outside of these dc pairs.

FINISHED MEASUREMENTS

Bust 32 (36, 40, 46, 49)"/81.5 (91.5, 101.5, 117, 124.5)cm

MATERIALS AND TOOLS

Misti Alpaca Tonos Pima Silk (83% Pima cotton/17% silk, 3.5oz/100 g = 327 yd/295m): 2 (3, 3, 4, 4) hanks—approx 654 (981, 981, 1308, 1308)yds/590 (885, 885, 1180, 1180)m of DK weight yarn; **3**

Crochet hook: 3.25mm (size D-3 U.S.)

6 buttons with shanks, approx 1/2"/13mm in diameter

Yarn needle

Sewing needle

Matching sewing thread

GAUGE (AFTER BLOCKING)

16 sts and 8 rows in Mini Ripple Pattern = 4"/10cm

Always take time to check your gauge.

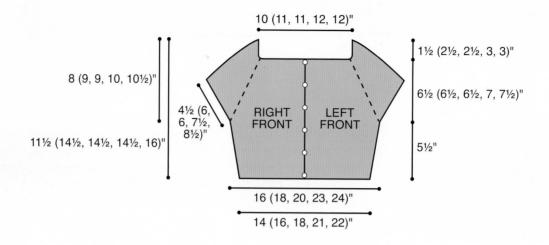

10 (11, 11, 12, 12)"

1½ (2½, 2½, 3, 3)"

8 (9, 9, 10, 10½)"

6½ (6½, 6½, 7, 7½)"

4½ (6, 6, 7½, 8½)"

RIGHT FRONT

LEFT FRONT

11½ (14½, 14½, 14½, 16)"

5½"

16 (18, 20, 23, 24)"

14 (16, 18, 21, 22)"

Instructions

Yoke

Ch 124 (152, 152, 176, 176).

ROW 1 (RS): Dc in 4th ch from hook, dc3tog over next 3 ch, [3 dc in next ch, dc3tog (Mini Ripple made)] 4 (5, 5, 6, 6) times, 2 dc in next ch, V in next ch, 2 dc in next ch, dc3tog over next 3 ch, work 3 (5, 5, 6, 6) Mini Ripples, 2 dc in next ch, V in next ch, 2 dc in next ch, dc3tog over next 3 ch, work 9 (10, 10, 12, 12) Mini Ripples, 2 dc in next ch, V in next ch, 2 dc in next ch, dc3tog, 3 (5, 5, 6, 6) Mini Ripples, 2 dc in next ch, V in next ch, 2 dc in next ch, dc3tog over next 3 ch, work 4 (5, 5, 6, 6) Mini Ripples, 2 dc in last ch, turn—125 (153,153, 177, 177) sts.

ROW 2: Ch 3, dc in first dc, dc3tog, work 4 (5, 5, 6, 6) Mini Ripples, 2 dc in next ch, dc in next dc, V in next V, dc in next dc, 2 dc in next dc, dc3tog over next 3, work 3 (5, 5, 6, 6) Mini Ripples, 2 dc in next dc, dc in next dc, V in next V, dc in next dc, 2 dc in next

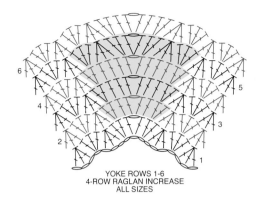

YOKE ROWS 1-6
4-ROW RAGLAN INCREASE
ALL SIZES

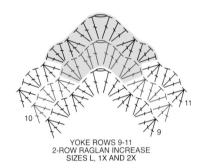

YOKE ROWS 9-11
2-ROW RAGLAN INCREASE
SIZES L, 1X AND 2X

dc, work 9 (10, 10, 12, 12) Mini Ripples, 2 dc in next dc, dc in next dc, V in next V, dc in next dc, 2 dc in next dc, dc3tog, work 3 (5, 5, 6, 6) Mini Ripples, 2 dc in next dc, dc in next dc, V in next V, dc in next dc, 2 dc in next dc, dc3tog, work 4 (5, 5, 6, 6) Mini Ripples, 2 dc in top of tch, turn—133 (161, 161, 185, 185) sts.

ROWS 3 AND 4: Cont in established patt, adding one more dc at each side of each V, which will add 8 sts in each row, ending with 149 (177, 177, 201, 201) sts.

ROW 5: Ch 3, dc in first dc, dc3tog, work 5 (6, 6, 7, 7) Mini Ripples, 2 dc in next dc, V in next V, 2 dc in next dc, dc3tog, work 5 (7, 7, 8, 8) Mini Ripples, 2 dc in next dc, V in next V, 2 dc in next dc, dc3tog, work 11 (12, 12, 14, 14) Mini Ripples, 2 dc in next dc, V in next V, 2 dc in next dc, dc3tog, work 5 (7, 7, 8, 8) Mini Ripples, 2 dc in next dc, V in next

V, 2 dc in next dc, dc3tog, work 5 (6, 6, 7, 7) Mini Ripples, 2 dc in top of tch, turn—157 (185, 185, 209, 209) sts.

ROW 6: Ch 3, dc in first dc, dc3tog, work 5 (6, 6, 7, 7) Mini Ripples, 2 dc in next dc, dc in next dc, V in next V, dc in next dc, 2 dc in neXt dc, dc3tog, work 5 (7, 7, 8, 8) Mini Ripples, 2 dc in next dc, dc in next dc, V in next V, dc in next dc, 2 dc in next dc, dc3tog, work 11 (12, 12, 14, 14) Mini Ripples, 2 dc in neXt dc, dc in next dc, V in next V, dc in next dc, 2 dc in next dc, dc3tog, work 5 (7, 7, 8, 8) Mini Ripples 2 dc in next dc, dc in next dc, V in next V, dc in next dc, 2 dc in next dc, dc3tog, work 5 (6, 6, 7, 7) Mini Ripples, 2 dc in top of tch, turn—165 (193, 193, 217, 217) sts.

ROWS 7 AND 8: Rep Rows 3 and 4, ending with 181 (209, 209, 233, 233) sts.

ROW 9: Ch 3, dc in first dc, dc3tog, work 6 (7,

7, 8, 8) Mini Ripples, 2 dc in next dc, V in next V, 2 dc in next dc, dc3tog, work 7 (9, 9, 10, 10) Mini Ripples, 2 dc in next dc, V in next V, 2 dc in next dc, dc3tog, work 13 (14, 14, 16, 16) Mini Ripples, 2 dc in next dc, V in next V, 2 dc in next dc, dc3tog, work 7 (9, 9, 10, 10) Mini Ripples, 2 dc in next dc, V in next V, 2 dc in next dc, dc3tog, work 6 (7, 7, 8, 8) Mini Ripples, 2 dc in top of tch, turn—189 (217, 217, 241, 241) sts.

Sizes S and M only:

ROW 10: Ch 3, dc in first dc, dc3tog, work 6 (7) Mini Ripples, 2 dc in next dc, dc in next dc, V in next V, dc in next dc, 2 dc in next dc, dc3tog, work 7 (9) Mini Ripples, 2 dc in next dc, dc in next dc, V in next V, dc in next dc, 2 dc in next dc, dc3tog, work 13 (14) Mini Ripples, 2 dc in next dc, dc in next dc, V in next V, dc in next dc, 2 dc in next dc, dc3tog, work 7 (9) Mini Ripples, 2 dc in next dc, dc in next dc, V in next V, dc in next dc, 2 dc in next dc, dc3tog, work 6 (7) Mini Ripples, 2 dc in top of tch, turn—197 (225) sts.

ROWS 11 AND 12: Rep Rows 3 and 4, ending with 213 (241) sts.

ROW 13: Cont in established patt completing 7 (8) Mini Ripples, 2 dc in next dc, V in next V, 2 dc in next dc, work 9 (11) Mini Ripples, 2 dc in next dc, dc3tog, work 15 (16) Mini Ripples, 2 dc in next dc, V in next V, 2 dc in next dc, work 9 Mini Ripples, 2 dc in next dc, V in next V, 2 dc in next dc, work 9 (11) Mini Ripples, 2 dc in next dc, V in next V, 2 dc in next dc, dc3tog, work 7 (8) Mini Ripples, 2 dc in top of tch, turn—221 (249) sts. Cont to Body.

Sizes L, 1X, and 2X only:

ROW 10: Ch 3, dc in first dc, dc3tog, work 7 (8, 8) Mini Ripples, 3 dc in next dc, 2 dc in next dc, V in next V, 2 dc in next dc, 3 dc in next dc, dc3tog, work 9 (10, 10) Mini Ripples, 3 dc in next dc, 2 dc in next dc, V in next V, 2

dc in next dc, 3 dc in next dc, dc3tog, work 14 (16, 16) Mini Ripples, 3 dc in next dc, 2 dc in next dc, V in next V, 2 dc in next dc, 3 dc in next dc, dc3tog, work 9 (10, 10) Mini Ripples, 3 dc in next dc, 2 dc in next dc, V in next V, 2 dc in next dc, 3 dc in next dc, dc3tog, work 7 (8, 8) Mini Ripples, 2 dc in top of tch, turn—241 (265, 265) sts.

ROW 11: Ch 3, dc in first dc, dc3tog, work 8 (9, 9) Mini Ripples, 2 dc in next dc, V in next V, 2 dc in next dc, dc3tog, work 11 (12, 12) Mini Ripples, 2 dc in next dc, V in next V, 2 dc in next dc, dc3tog, work 16 (18, 18) Mini Ripples, 2 dc in next dc, V in next V, 2 dc in next dc, dc3tog, work 11 (12, 12) Mini Ripples, 2 dc in next dc, V in next V, 2 dc in next dc, dc3tog, work 8 (9, 9) Mini Ripples, 2 dc in top of tch, turn—249 (273, 273) sts.

ROW 12: Ch 3, dc in first dc, dc3tog, work 8 (9, 9) Mini Ripples, 3 dc in next dc, 2 dc in next dc, V in next V, 2 dc in next dc, 3 dc in next dc, dc3tog, work 11 (12, 12) Mini Ripples, 3 dc in next dc, 2 dc in next dc, V in next V, 2 dc in next dc, 3 dc in next dc, dc3tog, work 16 (18, 18) Mini Ripples, 3 dc in next dc, 2

dc in next dc, V in next V, 2 dc in next dc, 3 dc in next dc, dc3tog, work 11 (12, 12) Mini Ripples, 3 dc in next dc, 2 dc in next dc, V in next V, 2 dc in next dc, 3 dc in next dc, dc3tog, work 8 (9, 9) Mini Ripples, 2 dc in top of tch, turn—273 (297, 297) sts.

ROW 13: Ch 3, dc in first dc, dc3tog, work 9 (10, 10) Mini Ripples, 2 dc in next dc, V in next V, 2 dc in next dc, dc3tog, work 13 (14, 14) Mini Ripples, 2 dc in next dc, V in next V, 2 dc in next dc, dc3tog, work 18 (20, 20) Mini Ripples, 2 dc in next dc, V in next V, 2 dc in next dc, dc3tog, work 13 (14, 14) Mini Ripples, 2 dc in next dc, V in next V, 2 dc in next dc, dc3tog, work 9 (10, 10) Mini Ripples, 2 dc in top of tch, turn—281 (305, 305) sts. Size L, cont to Body.

Size 1X only:

ROW 14: Ch 3, dc in first dc, dc3tog, work 10 Mini Ripples, 2 dc in next dc, dc in next dc, V in next V, dc in next dc, 2 dc in net dc, dc3tog, work 15 Mini Ripples, 2 dc in next dc, dc in next dc, V in next V, dc in next dc, 2 dc in next dc, dc3tog, work 20

Mini Ripples, 2 dc in net dc, dc in next dc, V in next V, dc in next dc, 2 dc in next dc, dc3tog, work 15 Mini Ripples 2 dc in next dc, dc in next dc, V in next V, dc in next dc, 2 dc in next dc, dc3tog, work 10 Mini Ripples, 2 dc in top of tch, turn—313 sts. Cont to Body.

Size 2X only:
ROW 14: Ch 3, dc in first dc, dc3tog, work 10 Mini Ripples, 3 dc in next dc, 2 dc in next dc, V in next V, 2 dc in next dc, 3 dc in next dc, dc3tog, work 14 Mini Ripples, 3 dc in next dc, 2 dc in next dc, V in next V, 2 dc in next dc, 3 dc in next dc, dc3tog, work 20

Mini Ripples, 3 dc in next dc, 2 dc in next dc, V in next V, 2 dc in next dc, 3 dc in next dc, dc3tog, work 14 Mini Ripples, 3 dc in next dc, 2 dc in next dc, V in next V, 2 dc in next dc, 3 dc in next dc, dc3tog, work 10 Mini Ripples, 2 dc in top of tch, turn—329 sts.
ROW 15: Ch 3, dc in first dc, dc3tog, work 11 Mini Ripples, 2 dc in next dc, V in next V, 2 dc in next dc, dc3tog, work 16 Mini Ripples, 2 dc in next dc, V in next V, 2 dc in next dc, dc3tog, work 22 Mini Ripples, 2 dc in next dc, V in next V, 2 dc in next dc, dc3tog, work 16 Mini Ripples, 2 dc in next dc, V in next V, 2 dc in next dc, dc3tog, work 11 Mini Ripples, 2 dc in top of tch, turn—337 sts. Cont to Body.

Body

221 (249, 281, 313, 337) sts are now on work. On the next row fronts will be joined to back forming sleeve openings, and sts will be added at underarm.

ROW 1: Ch 3, dc in first dc, dc3tog, work even in Mini Ripple Patt across right front to first dc of V, dc in first dc of V, ch 3 (5, 5, 7, 7), sk all sleeve sts to next V, sk next ch-1 sp of V, dc in 2nd dc of V on back, work even in Mini Ripple Patt across back to next V, dc in first dc of V, ch 3 (5, 5, 7, 7), sk all sleeve sts to next V, skip next ch-1 sp of V, dc in 2nd dc of V on left front, cont even in Mini Ripple Patt to end, 2 dc in top of tch, turn—127 (145, 161, 183, 193) sts. PM in center st of underarm.

ROW 2 (DEC ROW): *Work in patt across to dc section of underarm, dc in each dc to 1 dc before marker, dc3tog over next 3 dc, PM, dc in each rem dc of underarm, rep from * once, work in patt to end, turn—123 (141, 157, 179, 189) sts.

ROW 3: Cont working even in patt, working 1 dc in each dc at underarm.

ROWS 4–9: Rep Rows 2-3 (3 times)—111 (129, 145, 167, 177) sts.

ROWS 10 AND 11: Work even in patt—125 (143, 159, 185, 195) sts. Fasten off.

Bottom Trim

ROW 1: Ch 1, sc in first st, *ch 1, sc in next st, rep from * across, turn—61 (71, 79, 92, 97) ch-1 sps.

ROW 2: Ch 1, sc in first sc, *sc in next ch-1 sp, ch 1, rep from * across, sc in next ch-1 sp, sc in last sc, turn—60 (70, 78, 91, 96) ch-1 sps.

ROW 3: Ch 1, sc in first sc, ch 1, *sc in next ch-1 sp, ch 1, rep from * across, ending with sc in last sc, turn.

ROW 4: Rep Row 2. Do not fasten off. Rotate work 90° to work across left front edge.

Left Front Trim

ROW 1: Ch 1, sc in side of last sc made, ch 1, (sc, ch 1) over each row-end across left front edge, turn.

ROWS 2 AND 3: Rep Rows 2 and 3 of bottom trim. Fasten off.

Bottom Trim Continued

ROW 1: With RS facing, join yarn at bottom left-hand corner of left front, to work across bottom edge, ch 1, sc in first sc, ch 1, *sc in next ch-1 sp, ch 1, rep from * across, ending with sc in last sc. Do not fasten off. Rotate work 90° to work across right front edge.

Right Front Trim

Rep Row 1 of Left Front Trim.
PM 2 sts below top and 3 sts above bottom of last row. Place 4 markers evenly spaced between.

ROW 2 (BUTTONHOLE ROW): Ch 1, sc in first sc, *ch 2, sk next 2 sts, sc in next ST, [ch 1, sc in next ch-1 sp] to next marker, rep from * 4 times, ch 2, sk next 2 sts, sc in last st, turn. Note: the ch-2 will cause you to work a sc in a sc at times. When that happens, sc in next ch-1 sp and cont in patt.

ROW 3: Rep Row 3 of bottom trim. Fasten off.

Sleeve Trim

ROW 1: With RS facing, join yarn at bottom of sleeve, in "seam" st at left, ch 1, sc in same st, *ch 1, sc in next st, rep from * around sleeve, sl st in first sc.

RNDS 2–4: Sl st in next ch-1 sp, ch 1, sc in same sp, ch 1, (sc, ch 1) in each ch-1 sp around, sl st in first sc. Fasten off.
Rep on opposite Sleeve.

Finishing

With sewing needle and sewing thread, sew buttons to Left Front trim opposite buttonholes.

SHRUG HUG IS A CUTE wardrobe item for summer. What's interesting in this design is the small ripple pattern that creates visual interest on the surface. If you like the design but can't see yourself in something this short, lengthening it is easy.

Construction Details

Shaping with ripple patterns is a bit complex, because of the way stitches line up from one row to the next. The crucial thing is to make sure your stitch count keeps going up, as it must in the yoke portion of this pattern. Once the extra stitch counts at any increase point reaches 4, they are converted into a Mini Ripple pattern. To see how this is done, look closely at Rows 4 and 5 in the Yoke diagram on page 121.

Choosing Yarn

Any sock yarn will look great in this design. The subtly varying color and luxuriously soft Pima cotton are a strong part of the appeal. With all the marvelous sock yarns available, in a huge array of fibers and colors, this design could easily be made in several versions, long or short. It's a great project to polish your top-down skills.

Fit and Choosing Your Size

This garment has a very open square neck, a roomy fit at the bust line, and is more snug at the bottom. The neckline measures between 10 and 12"/25.4 and 30.5cm, but actually "wears" wider than this measurement as the caps of the sleeves tend to drape over the top of the shoulders.

   Because of the wide neckline, pick the size that's most suitable in neckline width according to the schematic. You want to avoid having the sweater fall off your shoulders or show your bra strap. Refer to the width measurement between bra straps that you took earlier, and note that across the shoulders the neckline will be about 2"/5cm wider than what is on the schematic. Now check to see if the neckline width that's right for you also gives you the right bust width. If not, use the lesson that follows and choose one of the options offered.

LESSON 15: Bust Alteration in Top-Down Design

We've covered bust alteration in other constructions and will now examine how it's done in a top-down, one-piece design. Recall that the sweater begins at the neckline, with increases made in the yoke as it progresses down to the bust and tops of the sleeves.

To enlarge the bust width, first determine exactly how many extra inches/centimeters you will need at the end of the yoke. If it's less than 2"/5cm total, an easy fix is to keep the yoke as is and add stitches on the first row of the Body. That row now reads:

ROW 1: Ch 3, dc in first dc, dc3tog, work even in Mini Ripple patt across right front to first dc of V, dc in first dc of V, **ch 3 (5, 5, 7, 7)**, sk all sleeve sts to next V, sk next ch-1 sp of V, dc in 2nd dc of V on back, work even in Mini Ripple patt across back to next V, dc in first dc of V, **ch 3 (5, 5, 7, 7)**, sk all sleeve sts to next V, skip next ch-1 sp of V, dc in 2nd dc of V on left front, cont even in Mini Ripple patt to end, 2 dc in top of tch, turn—127 (145, 161, 183, 193) sts. PM in center st of underarm.

Stitches are added in this row by making the chains specified (see **bold** numbers) *before* skipping the sleeve stitches. This happens in two spots on the row because stitches are added under each sleeve. Since gauge is 16 sts = 4"/10.2cm, it means that 4 stitches will give you an extra 1"/2.5cm. You can add 4 more chains at both spots and gain a total of 2"/5cm of body width. In subsequent rows, these stitches are not in the Mini Ripple pattern, but are plain dc stitches. For this reason, I don't recommend adding more than 4, as it may be visible and detract from the look of the sweater.

Another option is to make the size that does fit your bust, and then tighten the neckline after you're done. This is easily accomplished by working rows of single crochet edging all around the neckline, with decreases in each row. You can decrease up to 8 stitches in a row, spreading your decreases around evenly and as invisibly as possible. Try on the sweater after you've worked a couple of rows in this way, and continue until it sits with sufficient snugness around your neck and shoulders.

Yet a third option is to work additional rows, increasing in the same way as you have been in earlier rows. If you use this method, your yoke will be deeper, and this means the armhole will sit lower. This will not affect the fit, so long as you add no more than 1½"/3.8cm of depth, that is, up to 3 more rows.

You can use a combination of the first and last methods to add substantially to the bust width.

What if you want to tackle the option of adding more stitches as you work the yoke? In top-down sweaters, the increases are made at four points that delineate the front, back, and each sleeve of the sweater. In this pattern, those four corners consist of a V stitch, which separates the Mini Ripples that make up these four sections. If you look at any row in this pattern, you can find those four V stitches, and you can also see how the Mini Ripple counts are increasing as the rows progress. Since the sweater is a cardigan, it's begun at the center front edge, with the first V placed where one sleeve begins; the second V marks the end of that sleeve and the beginning of the back; the next V marks the end of the back and the beginning of the second sleeve, and the last V marks the end of the second sleeve and beginning of the opposite front piece.

In the pattern as written, increases are made at the rate of 8 sts per row, by adding 2 dc at each increase point. To increase more rapidly, you can add 4 dcs in the increase points, but only on the front. For example, here is row 2 of the pattern:

ROW 2: Ch 3, dc in first dc, dc3tog, work 4 (5, 5, 6, 6) Mini Ripples, 2 dc in next ch, dc in next dc, V in next V, dc in next dc, 2 dc in next dc, dc3tog over next 3, work 3 (5, 5, 6, 6) Mini Ripples, 2 dc in next dc, dc in next dc, V in next V, **2 dc in next dc**, 2 dc in next dc, work 9 (10, 10, 12, 12) Mini Ripples, 2 dc in next dc, **2 dc in next dc**, V in next V, dc in next dc, 2 dc in next dc, dc3tog, work 3 (5, 5, 6, 6) Mini Ripples, 2 dc in next dc, dc in next dc, V in next V, dc in next dc, 2 dc in next dc, dc3tog, work 4 (5, 5, 6, 6) Mini Ripples, 2 dc in top of tch.

The relevant points are in **bold** letters. At each of them you can make 2 dc instead of 1. Note that this will add stitches to the front only. If you do that in both rows 2 and 3, in your next round, convert the extra dc into Mini Ripples as in row 5 of the Yoke Rows 1-6 diagram on page 121. By continuing in this way, you can get a higher number of Mini Ripples to accommodate a larger bust.

Additional Alteration Ideas

Review the material in Shaping and Alteration 101 (page 34) to extend this sweater to any length you wish. Hopefully, you've already applied some of the lengthening lessons to other garments. Since this design fits very snugly under the bust, you can make it roomier in a longer version by decreasing more slowly than is done on the pattern as you work down to the waist and then increase again for the hip. The sleeves can be extended as well.

CREAM PUFF
circular yoke construction

Practice internal shaping techniques and work two different stitch patterns as you create this seamless one-piece garment in the round.

Stitch Patterns

❖ SHELL PATTERN

Ch a multiple of 6 plus 1 + 3 for tch.

Row 1: 2 dc in 4th ch from hook, dc5tog over next 5 ch, 5 dc in next ch, rep from * across, 3 dc in last ch, turn.

Row 2: Ch 3, FPdc2tog over next 2 sts (counts as FPdc3tog here and throughout), FPdc5tog over next 5 sts, 5 dc in top of next cluster, rep from * across to last 3 sts, FPdc3tog over last 3 sts, turn.

Row 3: Ch 3, 2 dc in first dc, *FPdc5tog over next 5 sts, 5 dc in top of next cluster, rep from * across to last st, 3 dc in tch, turn.

Rep Rows 2 and 3 for patt.

Note: Work last st of patt rep in tch. Keep loop after FPdc5tog tight.

❖ HDC/CL PATTERN

Row 1 (hdc row): Ch 2 (counts as hdc), hdc in each st across, turn.

Row 2 (CL row): Ch 3 (does not count as a st), CL over first and 2nd st, *CL over same st as 2nd leg of last CL and next st, rep from * across, ending in tch, dc in same tch.

Row 3 (hdc row): Ch 2 (counts as hdc), hdc in each st across, do not work in tch, turn.

Rep Rows 2 and 3 for patt.

For hdc rows, count the starting ch-2 as a st. In the row after the hdc row, work a st in the top of the tch to maintain st count.

Decreasing in hdc rows: When working randomly spaced decreases and increases, there are no exact stitch counts for where to place decreases. Make your decreases and increases anywhere in the row, spreading them out on the two front sections and back. Vary your placement of decreases and increases in subsequent rows so they don't line up directly over those made previously. There is no increasing or decreasing on CL rows.

FINISHED MEASUREMENTS

Bust 34 (37 1/2, 41 1/2, 46, 50)"/86.5 (95, 105.5, 117, 127)cm

Note about bust measurement: The style is meant to create an opening at the front, above a high waist. The front bands add 3"/7.6cm to the bust width.

MATERIALS AND TOOLS

Lion Brand Baby Alpaca (100% alpaca; 1.75oz/50g = 146yd/132m): 7 (9, 9, 11, 11) skeins, color Natural—approx 1022 (1314, 1314, 1606, 1606)yds/924 (1188, 1888, 1452, 1452)m of DK weight yarn; (3)

Crochet hook: 3.75mm (size F-5 U.S.)

One button approx 1"/2.5cm in diameter

Yarn needle

Sewing needle

Matching sewing thread

GAUGE (AFTER BLOCKING)

In Shell and Cluster Patterns, 4 pattern repeats = 5½"/14cm; 5 rows = 2"/5cm

In body pattern, 11 CL = 3"/7.6cm; 12 rows= 4½"/11.4cm

Always take time to check your gauge.

Special Abbreviations

Cluster (CL): [Yo, insert hook in next st, draw up a loop] twice, yo, draw yarn through 4 loops, yo, draw through 2 loops.

Tall Cluster (tall CL): [Yo (twice), insert hook in next st, draw up a loop, yo draw through 2 loops] twice, yo, draw through 4 loops, yo, draw through 2 loops.

Continued on next page

dec 1 hdc (special hdc2tog): Yo, [insert hook in next st] twice, draw up a loop, yo, draw yarn through 3 loops.

dc5tog: [Yo, insert hook in next st, yo, draw yarn through, yo, draw yarn through 2 loops] 5 times, yo, draw yarn through 6 loops.

dc5tog worked over next 4 sts: [Yo, insert hook in next st, draw up a loop, yo, draw yarn through 2 loops] twice, yo, insert hook in same st, draw up a loop, yo, draw yarn through 2 loops, [Yo, insert hook in next st, yo, draw yarn through, yo, draw yarn through 2 loops] twice, yo, draw yarn through 6 loops.

FPdc2tog: [Yo, insert hook around the post of next st, draw up a loop, yo, draw yarn through 2 loops] twice, yo, draw yarn through 3 loops.

FPdc3tog: [Yo, insert hook around the post of next st, draw up a loop, yo, draw yarn through 2 loops] 3 times, yo, draw yarn through 4 loops.

FPdc4tog: [Yo, insert hook around the post of next st, draw up a loop, yo, draw yarn through 2 loops] 4 times, yo, draw yarn through 5 loops.

FPdc5tog: [Yo, insert hook around the post of next st, draw up a loop, yo, draw yarn through 2 loops] 5 times, yo, draw yarn through 6 loops.

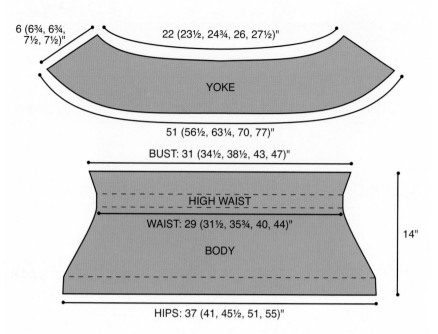

6 (6¾, 6¾, 7½, 7½)"

22 (23½, 24¾, 26, 27½)"

YOKE

51 (56½, 63¼, 70, 77)"

BUST: 31 (34½, 38½, 43, 47)"

HIGH WAIST

WAIST: 29 (31½, 35¾, 40, 44)"

BODY

14"

HIPS: 37 (41, 45½, 51, 55)"

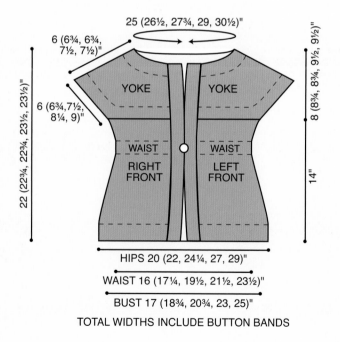

25 (26½, 27¾, 29, 30½)"

6 (6¾, 6¾, 7½, 7½)"

8 (8¾, 8¾, 9½, 9½)"

YOKE   YOKE

6 (6¾, 7½, 8¼, 9)"

22 (22¾, 22¾, 23½, 23½)"

WAIST   WAIST

RIGHT FRONT   LEFT FRONT

14"

HIPS 20 (22, 24¼, 27, 29)"

WAIST 16 (17¼, 19½, 21½, 23½)"

BUST 17 (18¾, 20¾, 23, 25)"

TOTAL WIDTHS INCLUDE BUTTON BANDS

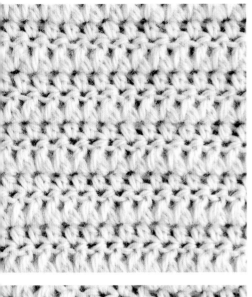

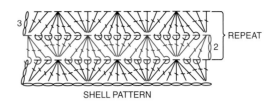

REPEAT

SHELL PATTERN

HDC/CLUSTER PATTERN

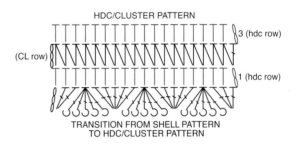

3 (hdc row)

(CL row)

1 (hdc row)

TRANSITION FROM SHELL PATTERN
TO HDC/CLUSTER PATTERN

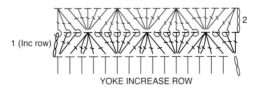

2

1 (Inc row)

YOKE INCREASE ROW

Instructions

Hip to High Waist Shaping

Ch 166 (184, 202, 226, 244).

Note: Row 1 is a WS row.

ROWS 1–5: Work in Shell Patt on 27 (30, 33, 37, 40) reps—164 (182, 200, 224, 242) sts.

ROW 6: Ch 2 (counts as hdc here and throughout), hdc in next 2 dc, *hdc2tog over top of CL and next dc**, hdc in next 4 dc, rep from * across, ending last rep at **, hdc in last 2 dc, turn—136 (151, 166, 186, 201) sts.

ROW 7: Work row 2 of Hdc/CL Patt—136 (151, 166, 186, 201) sts.

ROW 8: Ch 2, hdc in each st across, dec 3 (4, 4, 4, 4) times randomly spaced across, turn—133 (147, 162, 182, 197) sts.

ROWS 9–16: Rep rows 7 and 8 (4 times—121 (131, 146, 166, 181) sts at end of last row.

ROW 17: Work row 2 of Hdc/CL Patt.

ROW 18: Ch 2, hdc in each st across, dec 3 (3, 3, 4, 4) times randomly spaced across, turn—118 (128, 143, 162, 177) sts.

ROWS 19–26: Rep rows 17 and 18 (4 times— 106 (116, 131, 146, 161) sts at end of last row.

High Waist

ROW 27: Ch 3, 2 dc in first hdc, *dc5tog worked over next 4 sts (placing 2 dc in 2nd dc), 5 dc in next hdc, rep from * across, ending with 3 dc in tch—21 (23, 26, 29, 32) patt reps—127 (139, 157, 175, 193) sts.

ROWS 28 AND 29: Work rows 2 and 3 of shell/cluster pattern.

ROW 30: Ch 2, *hdc2tog over next 2 sts, hdc in next 4 dc, rep from * across to last 2 sts, hdc2tog over last 2 sts, turn—106 (116, 131, 146, 161) sts.

ROW 31: Work row 2 of Hdc/CL Patt.

ROW 32: Ch 2, hdc in each st across, inc (by working 2 hdc in 1 st) 3 (3, 3, 4, 4) times randomly spaced across, turn—109 (119, 134, 150, 165) sts.

ROWS 33–34: Rep rows 31 and 32 once—112 (122, 137, 154, 169) sts.

ROW 35: Work row 2 of Hdc/CL Patt.

ROW 36: Ch 2, hdc in each st across, inc 1 hdc 2 (4, 4, 4, 4) times randomly spaced across, turn—114 (126, 141, 158, 173) sts.

Sizes L, 1X, and 2X only:

ROW 37: Ch 2, hdc in each st across, turn.

ROW 38: Work row 2 of Hdc/CL Patt.

Mark RS of garment. Row 1 on bottom edge should be a WS row, so that the scalloped edge curls in.

Right Sleeve Opening

With RS facing, sk first 25 (25, 30, 35, 40) sts from beg of last row. PM in next st. Join yarn in marked st, ch 48 (54, 60, 66, 72), sk next 4 (5, 5, 6, 6) sts, sl st in next st. Fasten off.

Left Sleeve Opening

With WS facing, sk first 24 (24, 29, 34, 39) sts from end of last row. PM in next st. Join yarn in marked st, ch 48 (54, 60, 66, 72), sk next 4 (5, 5, 6, 6) sts, sl st in next st. Fasten off.

Yoke

ROW 1: Ch 3, 2 dc in first hdc, *dc5tog worked across next 4 sts (placing 2 dc in 2nd dc), 5 dc in next hdc*, rep from * 4 (4, 5, 6, 7) times, [5 dc in next ch, dc5tog over next 5 ch] 8 (9, 10, 11, 12) times, rep from * to * 11 (13, 14, 15, 16) times (across back), [5 dc in next ch, dc5tog over next 5 ch] 8 (9, 10, 11, 12) times, rep from * to * 5 (5, 6, 7, 8) times, 3 dc in tch, turn–37 (41, 46, 51, 56) patt reps; 223 (247, 277, 307, 337) sts.

ROW 2: Work even in row 2 of Shell/Cluster Patt.

ROW 3: Ch 3, 2 dc in first dc, *FPdc5tog worked over next 5 sts, 4 dc in next st, rep from * across, ending with 3 dc in tch, turn—187 (207, 232, 257, 282) sts.

ROW 4: Ch 3, FPdc2tog over next 2 sts, *4 dc in next st, FPdc4tog over next 4 sts, rep from * across, ending with FPdc3tog over last 3 sts, turn.

ROW 5: Ch 3, 2 dc in first dc, *FPdc4tog over next 4 sts, 4 dc in next st, rep from * across, ending with 3 dc in tch, turn.

ROW 6: Ch 3, FPdc2tog over next 2 sts, *3 dc in next st, dc4tog over next 4 sts, rep from * across, FPdc3tog over last 3 sts, turn—149 (165, 185, 205, 225) sts

ROW 7: Ch 3, 2 dc in first st, *FPdc3tog over next 3 sts, 3 dc in next st, rep from * across, ending with 3 dc in tch, turn.

ROW 8: Ch 2, hdc in next 2 sts, *hdc2tog over next 2 sts, hdc in next 2 sts, rep from * across to last within 2 sts, hdc in each of last 2 sts, turn—113 (125, 140, 155, 170) sts.

ROW 9: Work row 2 of Hdc/CL patt.

ROW 10: Ch 2, hdc in each st across, dec 1 hdc 9 (7, 10, 10, 14) times randomly spaced across, turn—104 (118, 130, 145, 156) sts.

Back Neck Shaping

ROW 11: Ch 3, work 26 (29, 32, 36, 39) CL, work 52 (60, 66, 73, 78) Tall CL, work 26 (29, 32, 36, 39) CL, turn.

ROW 12: Ch 2, hdc in each st across, dec 1 hdc 7 (7, 11, 10, 13) times randomly spaced across, turn—97 (111, 119, 135, 143) sts.

Sizes M, L, 1X, and 2 X only:

ROW 13: Ch 3, work 27 (29, 33, 35) CL, work 57 (61, 69, 73) Tall CL, work 27 (29, 33, 35) CL, turn.

ROW 14: Ch 2, hdc in each st across, dec 1 hdc 8 (10, 10, 12) times randomly spaced across, turn—103 (109, 125, 131) sts.

ROW 15: Ch 3, work 25 (27, 31, 32) CL, work 53 (55, 63, 67) Tall CL, work 25 (27, 31, 32) CL, turn.

Sizes 1X and 2 X only:

ROW 16: Ch 2, hdc in each st across, dec 1 hdc 10 times randomly spaced across, turn—115 (121) sts.

ROW 17: Ch 3, work 28 (30) CL, work 59 (61) Tall CL, work 28 (30) CL, turn.

All Sizes:

ROW 13 (16, 16, 18, 18): Work in Shell Patt across—16 (17, 18, 19, 20) patt reps—97 (103, 109, 115, 121) sts.

ROW 14 (17, 17, 19, 19): Ch 3, FPdc2tog over next 2 sts, *4 dc in next st, FPdc5tog over next 5 sts, rep from * across, FPdc3tog over last 3 sts—81 (86, 91, 96, 101) sts

ROW 15 (18, 18, 20, 20): Ch 3, 2 dc in first st, *FPdc4tog over next 4 sts, 4 dc in next st, rep from * across, 3 dc in tch, turn.

ROW 16 (19, 19, 21, 21): Ch 3, FPdc2tog over next 2 sts, *3 dc in next st, FPdc4tog over next 4 sts, rep from * across, dc3tog over last 3 sts. Fasten off—65 (69, 73, 77, 81) sts.

Finishing

Right Sleeve Edging:
With RS facing, join yarn at edge of front yoke, sl st across underarm to edge of back yoke. Fasten off.

Left Sleeve Edging:
With RS facing, join yarn at edge of back yoke, sl st across underarm to edge of front yoke. Fasten off.

Right Front Border:
PM 1 1/2"/3.8cm above bottom edge on right front edge, *PM 1 1/2"/3.8cm above last marker, rep from * across to front edge, adjusting as necessary to mark a total of 13 spaces.
ROW 1: With RS facing, join yarn at bottom edge of right front edge, work row 1 of Shell Patt across Right Front edge, working 1 patt rep between each marker, turn—13 patt reps.
ROWS 2 AND 3: Work Rows 2 and 3 of Shell Patt. Fasten off.

Left Front Border:
Work same as right front border, starting at top edge of Left Front edge.
    With sewing needle and thread, sew button to Left Front border, at level of waistband. Use space between sts on Right Front border for buttonhole.

Neck Trim (optional):
To create a smaller neck opening, with RS facing, work a row of sl st across top edge of neck opening. Fasten off.

CREAM PUFF IS A feminine design that can teach you many things about creating a one-piece, form-fitting garment. It's great for layering and can be used in your wardrobe like a vest, over a top with short sleeves or long. If you think the empire waist is only for teens, move it down to waist level—an easy alteration.

Construction Details

This round-yoke, one-piece design is worked from the bottom up. When working in the round, you don't have to think about seams or decreasing at side edges. All the shaping is done internally, within the row. This gives you a lot of freedom when adding or subtracting stitches and will make any width alterations easier.

A garment with internal shaping looks different laid flat than a garment shaped at the sides. The front edges at their narrowest will roll apart when flat, but will extend around the body when worn.

I like the way these two stitch patterns balance each other. For convenience of discussion, let's identify the two stitch patterns as plain and fancy, the plain being the Hdc/Cl pattern and the fancy being the Shell Pattern. Most of the shaping of the torso occurs on the plain rows. The decreases from the bottom of the sweater to the waist are handled by dispersing them at your discretion on the fronts and back. In the Yoke section, the fancy pattern is shaped by changing the size of the Pattern Repeat, decreasing it by one stitch, from 6, to 5, then 4 by the final row of fancy pattern.

One more element is worth bringing to your attention. On the back of the sweater near the neckline, there are 1 or 2 plain rows with taller stitches. These build the back neck higher than the front, as is recommended for good fit. Knitters often use short rows to accomplish this. I'm all for short rows when they work, but in crochet we have many other options, and this is a perfect one for fine shaping.

Choosing Yarn

This pattern can be made in a variety of DK yarns. The alpaca used in the model keeps the garment light in weight. A nice merino will bring out the dimensional stitches even more, while a yarn with a bit of fuzz will emphasize the frothy character of this design—perfect for a teenager or twenty-something!

Fit and Choosing Your Size

Cream Puff is meant for a snug fit, but since it closes at only one point, below the bust, it has plenty of built-in ease. Choose the size that best matches your finished bust width, taking into account that there will be about 3 to 4"/7.6 to 10.2cm open in the front. In other words, look at the given bust widths and add that 3 to 4"/7.6 to 10.2cm to it, then compare that figure to the finished bust width you prefer.

LESSON 16: Length And Waist Alterations

Length can be added or subtracted on this garment, but be aware that you will need to put button bands on the front edges. This will work out fine if your end length is divisible by 1½"/3.8cm, the length of the pattern repeat (PR) used in the button bands.

CHANGING WAIST PLACEMENT

If you prefer a lower waistline, follow the procedures outlined in Shaping and Alteration 101 (page 34), and also, take a look at Lesson 6: Altering Length and Waist Placement (page 77). This alteration is a good option for those whose bust line sits low on the torso. You can move the high waist down to your natural waist and even eliminate the fancy pattern altogether in that area if you like. If you want the waist narrower than the measurement in the pattern, decrease more stitches in the hip-to-waist section of the pattern, distributing the decreases evenly over the decrease rows in this area. Then increase as necessary to arrive at full bust width where it occurs on your body, referring to your waist-to-full bust measurement.

LESSON 17: Master Class In Bust Alteration

Here is another excellent bust-line alteration. To widen the bust, you can begin by adding stitches to plain rows above the waist. To make the conversion to the fancy pattern easy, you want the total number of added stitches to be a multiple of 10. When you get to the armhole, you can add a few additional stitches there if your width is not yet adequate—but be sure to end with a stitch count that is divisible by 5. In the row that starts the yoke, you will be converting the stitches to the fancy pattern.

When you begin the yoke, distribute the extra repetitions of the fancy pattern on the back and front of the sweater. You can put one on each front piece and one or two on the back, for example. You do this in the rows labeled Right Sleeve Opening and Left Sleeve Opening, which read as follows:

Right Sleeve Opening:
With RS facing, sk first **25 (25, 30, 35, 40)** sts from beg of last row. Place marker in next st. Join yarn in marked st, ch 48 (54, 60, 66, 72), sk next 4 (5, 5, 6, 6) sts, sl st in next st. Fasten off.

Left Sleeve Opening:
With WS facing, sk first **24 (24, 29, 34, 39)** sts from end of last row. Place marker in next st. Join yarn in marked st, ch 48 (54, 60, 66, 72), sk next 4 (5, 5, 6, 6) sts, sl st in next st. Fasten off.

When counting the stitches shown in **bold**, add 5 stitches to the count on both left and right before placing your marker. This will place one of the additional PR on each front piece. Any remaining extra stitches will end up on the back.

After making this alteration, if your new PR count matches any of the other sizes, you can follow the pattern for that size for the rest of the yoke. It may need no adjustment at all; check the neck circumference on the size that conforms to your new PR count and see. Remember that the garment is open at the neck, and there will be another 2"/5cm of open space in the front neck. If you feel the neck measurement will be too wide for you, add decreases in the yoke (after the fancy pattern) on the plain rows near the end of the pattern. The decreases will allow you to arrive at the stitch count for a smaller neckline.

Acknowledgments

MY THANKS to the following: my friend, designer Leslie Johnson, for her excellent advice and encouragement; also to my friend, designer Lisa Daehlin, for her unflagging support; to the incomparable contract crocheter Nancy Smith; and to Kate Epstein, my agent, for wisely seeing me through this endeavor. I would also like to thank my editor at Lark Crafts, Valerie Van Arsdale Shrader, for her patience and intelligence, and my technical editor, Karen Manthey, who brought her superior skills to these patterns. Stylist Jodi Kahn and photographer Scott Jones allowed me to sit in on photo sessions and did a spectacular job of showing these garments at their best, as did the local beauties of Larchmont who modeled them.

I'm also grateful to the following companies who generously donated yarn for the ten garments in *Custom Crocheted Sweaters*:

❖ **Classic Elite Yarns**
  (122 Western Avenue, Lowell, MA 01851;
  978-453-2837; www.classiceliteyarns.com)

❖ **Crystal Palace Yarns**

❖ **Done Roving Farms Yarns**

❖ **Knit Picks**

❖ **Lion Brand Yarn**

❖ **Lorna's Laces**

❖ **Louet**

❖ **Misti Alpaca**

❖ **The Skacel Collection (Zitron)**

❖ **Tahki Stacy Charles, Inc. (Filatura di Crosa)**

Author Biography

DORA OHRENSTEIN first began crocheting during the Age of Aquarius, that is, around 1971, while living on a houseboat in Amsterdam. She then put crochet aside to pursue a career as a singer for the next 30 years, enjoying considerable success in classical music, touring all over the globe as the singer of the Philip Glass Ensemble, and making many recordings. In 2004 she picked up the hook again and has been publishing designs and articles ever since. This is Dora's second book with Lark Crafts; her first, *Creating Crochet Fabric*, was nominated for a Flamie award in 2011. Her online magazine *Crochet Insider* (www.crochetinsider.com), is one of the most admired and widely-read craft sites on the Web.

Photo by Simon Surowicz

Charts

Stitch Key

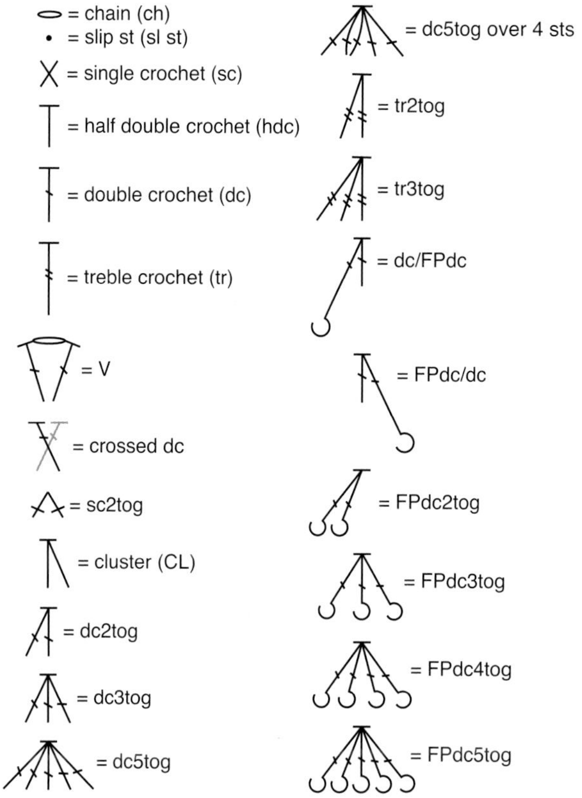

⬭ = chain (ch)
• = slip st (sl st)
X = single crochet (sc)
T = half double crochet (hdc)
T = double crochet (dc)
T = treble crochet (tr)
= V
= crossed dc
= sc2tog
= cluster (CL)
= dc2tog
= dc3tog
= dc5tog

= dc5tog over 4 sts
= tr2tog
= tr3tog
= dc/FPdc
= FPdc/dc
= FPdc2tog
= FPdc3tog
= FPdc4tog
= FPdc5tog

Metric Conversion Chart

1/8"	3 mm	2½"	6.4 cm	11"	27.9 cm	19½"	49.5 cm	28"	71.1 cm
3/16"	5 mm	3"	7.6 cm	11½"	29.2 cm	20"	50.8 cm	28½"	72.4 cm
1/4"	6 mm	3½"	8.9 cm	12"	30.5 cm	20½"	52.0 cm	29"	73.7 cm
5/16"	8 mm	4"	10.2 cm	12½"	31.8 cm	21"	53.3 cm	29½"	74.9 cm
3/8"	9.5 mm	4½"	11.4 cm	13"	33.0 cm	21½"	54.6 cm	30 "	76.2 cm
7/16"	1.1 cm	5"	12.7 cm	13½"	34.3 cm	22"	55.0 cm	30½"	77.5 cm
1/2"	1.3 cm	5½"	14.0 cm	14"	35.6 cm	22½"	57.2 cm	31"	78.7 cm
9/16"	1.4 cm	6"	15.2 cm	14½"	36.8 cm	23"	58.4 cm	31½"	80.0 cm
5/8"	1.6 cm	6½"	16.5 cm	15"	38.1 cm	23½"	59.7 cm	32"	81.3 cm
11/16"	1.7 cm	7"	17.8 cm	15½	39.4 cm	24"	61.0 cm	32½"	82.6 cm
3/4"	1.9 cm	7½"	19.0 cm	16"	40.6 cm	24½"	62.2 cm	33"	83.8 cm
13/16"	2.1 cm	8"	20.3 cm	16½"	41.9 cm	25"	63.5 cm	33½"	85.0 cm
7/8"	2.2 cm	8½"	21.6 cm	17"	43.2 cm	25½"	64.8 cm	34"	86.4 cm
15/16"	2.4 cm	9¼"	22.9 cm	17½"	44.5 cm	26"	66.0 cm	34½"	87.6 cm
1"	2.5 cm	9½"	24.1 cm	18"	45.7 cm	26½"	67.3 cm	35"	88.9 cm
1½"	3.8 cm	10"	25.4 cm	18½"	47.0 cm	27"	68.6 cm	35½"	90.2 cm
2"	5.0 cm	10½"	26.7 cm	19"	48.3 cm	27½"	69.9 cm	36"	91.4 cm

Crochet Abbreviations

ABBR	DESCRIPTION	ABBR	DESCRIPTION	ABBR	DESCRIPTION
[ ]	work instructions within brackets as many times as directed	dc2tog	double crochet 2 stitches together	p	picot
( )	work instructions within parentheses as many times as directed	dec	decrease/decreases/decreasing	pat(s) or patt	patterns
* *	repeat instructions between asterisks as many times as directed or repeat from a given set of instructions	dtr	double treble	PM	place marker
*	repeat instructions following the single asterisk as directed	fl	front loop(s)	pop	popcorn
"	inches	foll	follow/follows/following	prev	previous
alt	alternate	FP	front post	rem	remain/remaining
approx	approximately	FPdc	front post double crochet	rep	repeat(s)
beg	beginning	FPsc	front post single crochet	rnd(s)	round(s)
bet	between	FPtr	front post treble crochet	RS	right side
BL	back loop(s)	fl	front loop(s)	sc	single crochet
bo	bobble	foll	follow/follows/following	sc2tog	single crochet 2 stitches together
BP	back post	FP	front post	sk	skip
BPdc	back post double crochet	FPdc	front post double crochet	sl st	slip stitch
BPsc	back post single crochet	FPsc	front post single crochet	sp(s)	space(s)
BPtr	back post treble crochet	FPtr	front post treble crochet	st(s)	stitch(es)
CA	color A	g	grams	tbl	through back loop
CB	color B	hdc	half double crochet	tch	turning chain
CC	contrasting color	inc	increase/increases/increasing	tog	together
ch	chain stitch	invdec	invisible decrease	tr	treble crochet
ch-	refers to chain or space previously made; e.g., ch-1 space	lp(s)	loop(s)	trtr	triple treble crochet
ch-sp	chain space	m	meters	WS	wrong side
CL	cluster	MC	main color	yd(s)	yard(s)
cm	centimeter(s)	mm	millimeter(s)	yo	yarn over
cont	continue	mr	make ring	yoh	yarn over hook
dc	double crochet	oz	ounce(s)		

Yarn Weight Chart

YARN WEIGHT SYMBOL & CATEGORY NAMES	0 lace	1 super fine	2 fine	3 light	4 medium	5 bulky	6 super bulky
TYPE OF YARNS IN CATEGORY	Fingering 10-count crochet thread	Fingering, Baby	Sport, Sock	DK, Light Worsted	Worsted, Afghan, Aran	Chunky, Craft, Rug	Bulky, Roving

Source: Craft Yarn Council of America's www.YarnStandards.com

Regional Crochet Abbreviations

ABBR	U.S. TERM	ABBR	U.K./AUS TERM
sl st	slip st	sc	single crochet
sc	single crochet	dc	double crochet
hdc	half double crochet	htr	half treble crochet
dc	double crochet	tr	treble crochet
tr	treble crochet	dtr	double treble crochet
dtr	double treble crochet	trip tr or trtr	triple treble crochet
trtr	triple treble crochet	qtr	quadruple treble crochet
rev sc	reverse single crochet	rev dc	reverse double crochet
yo	yarn over	yoh	yarn over hook

Index